ACCLAIM FOR FAILURE IS NOT AN OPTION

"If you're at or near retirement, this is a must read. *Failure Is Not an Option* provides a compass for making the most of the second half of your financial journey. After reading David Rosell's book, you'll want to explore all that life has to offer."
—*Charles R. Schwab, Jr.*

"David Rosell's guide to retirement planning shows you not only how to get your finances in order, but also how to bring meaning and purpose to these very special years."
—*Ken Blanchard, co-author of* The One Minute Manager® *and* Trust Works!

"This powerful, practical book gives you a step-by-step guide to retiring in comfort and never worrying about money again."
—*Brian Tracy, author,* Change Your Thinking, Change Your Life

"I thought I would be reading another financial book. It didn't take long to realize that I was instead reading a book about life's grand journeys, and how getting the financial part right compliments our higher aspirations. I am not yet 'on the descent' but David Rosell has challenged me to prepare for that time in my life. He has done so in a way that not only offers profound financial planning advice (which he certainly does) but keeps things in perspective of what life is all about. Read the book, follow the advice, and buy a copy for someone you care about!"
—*Jeff Shore, sales expert and author of* Be Bold and Win the Sale

"*The Road Less Traveled* meets *Think and Grow Rich.* Achieving greatness in your retirement years can now be available to all of us after reading *Failure Is Not an Option.*"
—*Don Yaeger,* New York Times *bestselling author, former associate editor of* Sports Illustrated

"Wow! What an exciting and refreshing read in an ever-growing sea of mundane retirement books. *Failure Is Not an Option* combines the spirit of my audio program *Making Your Life an Adventure* and the win-win philosophy of my bestseller *Secrets of Power Negotiating.* This expert guided tour of the retirement you've always imagined is for every successful baby boomer and anyone who wants to live the dream."
—*Roger Dawson, author and Hall of Fame speaker*

"Our financial journey lasts a lifetime and is made up of two parts: Working years and retirement years. While our working years get us halfway to our destination, David's book is a step-by-step guide on planning our retirement years to successfully complete the trip in comfort. It should be mandatory reading for everyone 30 and above."
—*Jim Ruff, president, OppenheimerFunds Distributors, Inc. (Retired)*

"This book brings important financial lessons to life using highly entertaining and insightful travel stories."
—*Dan Sullivan, president, The Strategic Coach Inc.*

"Through engaging real-life travelogues and practical advice, David Rosell charts a clear and defined course to successful retirement. Entrepreneurs like me understand that the "failure is not an option" mantra is a necessary component of survival. David's book provides the recipe for financial success that we all need to not just survive in retirement, but to thrive. I'll lift a glass to that."

—*Gary D. Fish, Founder and CEO, Deschutes Brewery, Inc.*

"Failure is not an option is not just a catch phrase; it is a concept of life fulfillment for all of us. Being in the fourth quarter of my own journey, I believe David Rosell's wisdom is so critical to embrace for the second half of life that I am sharing it with all of my children and grand-children as they climb toward their own summits, yearning for achievement and financial independence."

—*Denis Waitley, author* Seeds of Greatness

FAILURE IS
NOT
AN OPTION

Creating Certainty
In the Uncertainty of Retirement

David Rosell

Failure Is Not an Option:
Creating Certainty in the Uncertainty of Retirement
© 2013 by David Rosell

ISBN: 978-0-9893881-0-8

Cover design by Lieve Maas
Cover photo by Jill Rosell

Published by
Incubation Press
Bend, OR
Incubationpress.com

To Grandma Ruth who crossed over before this project could be completed. Your contribution to my life has been priceless. I love you up the sky and down again.

And to every person, young and old, who dreams of becoming financially independent and building a happy, successful and rewarding life.

The goal of climbing big, dangerous mountains should be to attain some sort of spiritual and personal growth, but this won't happen if you compromise away the entire process.

—Yvon Chouinard

ACKNOWLEDGMENTS

This book is the product of many people's time, energy and input. I would like to express my gratitude to the many people who have supported and encouraged me.
Thanks go out to …

My wife Jill, and **children Sophie** and **Jack.** Of all who walk the earth, you are most precious to me. Jill, I couldn't have found a better friend or partner to share this journey with. You have been an inspiration for my book and your cover photo is absolutely beautiful. Sophie and Jack, your growth provides a constant source of joy and pride. May your life be filled with happiness and adventure. I know you will continue to appreciate the differences in people around the globe and make this world an even better place.

My parents, who always believed that I could do anything I put my mind to. You are the reason I am here. Dad, thanks for your significant financial and life lessons. Mom, thanks for being the world's greatest D&S Mom. I literally couldn't have run my early driveway sealing business without you.

Ann Golden Eglé for teaching me that great things are born from tiny sparks of inspiration, as well as about how to find the adventure of a six-month international sojourn during the work week.

Mona Delfino, my spiritual guide and sister from another mother (and father). The writing of your book inspired me to take action and do the same.

My business mentor and friend **Robert Berman,** who has shaped my practice in countless ways and taught me that the secret of success is consistency of purpose.

Jim Lee, a gentle and generous soul who is my mentor in business and, more importantly, in life.

My colleague **Brenna Hasty,** whose cheerful, friendly and positive demeanor helps to maintain the culture of my practice. Thank you for consistently providing the highest level of service to our clients. To **Amy Moser,** for eleven years of enthusiasm, dependability and laughs. Cheers to **caffeine,** my companion through many long nights of writing.

Linden Gross, whose guidance, coaching, editing and commitment to collaboration helped me turn 10 years of travel journals and a career of influential financial lessons into a comprehensible and fun read. To **Lieve Maas,** whose talents and creativity led to a handsome book design. To my friend and client **Ray Warrington** and his spirited friend **Diane Elliot,** for climbing to the top of Mt. Bachelor for the cover shoot.

My fellow foul-weather adventurers in the book who helped to shape my greatest memories of freedom and folly. May we always flee rhinos together.

My clients. I thank you from the bottom of my heart. It is because of you and your achievements that I have been motivated to write this book.

Lastly, to you the reader. I hope that you have at least half as much fun in the reading of this adventure/financial book as I've had in the writing. May you keep your dreams alive and live the life you have always imagined.

Contents

Chapter 1

You Have to Plan for the Second Half of the Journey

There are no shortcuts to any place worth going.

—Beverly Sills

Imagine that you're at Mt. Everest Base Camp and you've come across a group of mountaineers about to start their expedition to the summit. "What's your ultimate goal?" you ask them.

How would they answer?

If you're like most people, you probably assume that their ultimate goal is getting to the top.

As you're about to find out in this chapter, you'd be wrong.

"So what?" you're probably saying to yourself. "I'm not setting out to climb Mt. Everest."

That may be. However, your climb toward financial independence could make ascending Mt. Everest look like a stroll if you don't get it right. Failure is not an option.

That's a lesson I would discover early on.

REACHING FOR THE HEIGHTS

It was the adventure of a lifetime as I set off for Kathmandu, Nepal, in 1992 for a 21-day self-guided trek. My travel agent informed me I could fly Pakistan International Airways with a layover in Karachi or for the same price fly one of the world's most respected and luxurious airlines, Cathay Pacific, through Singapore. She steered me toward the latter for obvious reasons, but I opted for Pakistan as it could only add to the adventure. As I entered the aging 747 at John F. Kennedy International Airport, the ethnic and cultural diversity immediately conveyed that I was already in Pakistan. Repetitive strains of Bollywood-style music whined incessantly through the plane's speakers. The cabin was permeated with a highly seasoned, spicy scent of coriander, curry and dhal. The passengers were all decked out in their traditional dress of colorful, loose pajama-like trousers with long tunics.

Camel ride in Karachi, Pakistan.

After what seemed like days but was probably closer to 24 hours, I reached Karachi. The overnight layover allowed me to play tourist for a day in Pakistan's largest city of 32 million people. My escapades that day included riding a camel on the black sand beaches of this polluted seaport and visiting a mosque. I quickly concluded that Pakistan was as Third World as any developing country could be.

When I returned to my hotel room, I found a note posted on my door.

Mr. Rosell,
There is a military coup here in Pakistan. You are booked
on the next flight out to Kathmandu.

Amazed that our State Department had even known to contact me, I packed and immediately returned to the airport to embark on the next leg of my journey.

Upon boarding the plane for Kathmandu, I gravitated to the only other westerner on board. Ashley Turberfield was from Stratford-upon-Avon, the small English township Shakespeare had called home. We quickly struck up a conversation and learned that we had a great deal in common. Not only were we the same age, we shared the same goal: to reach the summit pass of Thorong La, which at 17,769 feet is the highest point on the 155-mile Annapurna Circuit. My life has always been a series of serendipitous events and this was no exception. Ashley would not only become my climbing partner over the next month, but a lifelong friend who would attend my wedding years later and eventually marry my wife's maid of honor.

As the plane descended into Kathmandu Valley, we could see the remnants of the Pakistan Airlines Airbus that had crashed on approach just weeks earlier. After such an action-packed introduction to Central Asia, touching down safely was downright delightful.

My new travel partner and I left the airport together. Filled with trepidation, we walked the discombobulated streets of Kathmandu in search of a place to spend the night. Our *Lonely Planet* guidebook eventually took us to The Chalet, a small guesthouse located in the hills overlooking the incredibly picturesque, yet ramshackle city.

The next morning we agreed to embark on our trek together. We wandered through the tourist district of Thamel to get a sense for the capital city and begin planning our expedition, all the while dodging cars that whizzed by at an uncomfortably close distance. We felt as if we had just been cast in the movie *Raiders of the Lost Ark*.

There is little else that has the intense power to overload all of one's senses as a stroll through the streets of Kathmandu. For starters, the smells can be both tantalizing and unbearable— aromas of turmeric and coriander billow out from the powdery burlap sacks of an elderly man grinding spices while a group of men smoking cheap Nepali cigarettes crouch on the curb to watch a cow getting slaughtered on the streets. Meanwhile, a woman washes her dishes and her children's clothes from a spigot, packs of flea-infested dogs roam the streets, and a man with missing appendages sells Gurkha army knives. Upon witnessing a dead body being cremated on the bank of the holy Bagmati River, we opted for a timeout back at our guesthouse.

Downtown Kathmandu.

By the time we entered a bus for the five-hour ride to Besi-sahar where our trek would begin, my stomach had started to do battle with the culinary delights of Kathmandu. An hour into the ride, with no bathroom anywhere close, my digestive tract suddenly surrendered. In a moment of sheer panic, I rushed up front to get the bus driver's attention. Using a new form of sign language, I succeeded in getting him to pull the bus over. As I ran out, an entire busload of Nepalese eyes shifted to the windows to see what this crazy American was doing. Unfortunately for me, there were no trees or obstacles to hide behind. There was nothing but an endless sea of tundra with the Himalayas dominating the horizon. So I had to answer the call of nature and my exploding bowels in full view of my audience. Embarrassing doesn't begin to describe the experience.

The rest of the ride was downright miserable because of details best left out, but when the world's tallest mountains came into view my focus shifted. Ashley and I were mesmerized by the snowcapped Himalayas that stretched into the deep blue skies. We had never experienced such enchanted beauty. The majesty was beyond anything I could have imagined.

GETTING TO THE TOP

Our 21-day expedition began the next morning. This would be the longest and most mentally and physically challenging trek of my life. Previous explorations had been limited to four or five days in the Southern Alps of New Zealand or overnight trips in the Rockies and Adirondacks. But our packs were organized and our course plotted on our detailed map. It was time to get started.

I spent much of the first week thinking about the summit. Reaching 5,416 meters (17,769 feet—higher than Mont Blanc, Europe's highest mountain) was a daunting prospect. *Will I be able to climb up so high?* I asked myself again and again. *Will the weather be good enough? Will it be bitter cold? What about altitude sickness or equipment failure?* For the first few days I kept saying to myself, *If I turned around right now it would only be a few days back rather than a few more weeks if I continue on.*

Happily, by the time we got to Dharapani, just 72 hours later, much of my anxiousness had turned into exhilaration. The serenity of this scenic mountain village surrounded with lush green subtropical valleys completely eclipsed the noise and chaos of Kathmandu. The people, predominantly Hindus, living in the lower elevations have sculpted terraces into the steep mountain slopes enabling them to farm the land. The rivers around the area, sourced from vast glaciers, help sustain life in the surrounding communities.

As we ascended to higher elevations the people became predominantly Tibetan Buddhist. They were so peaceful and calm. One could see the kindness in their eyes. They would put their hands together and say "Namaste" as we passed by them on the sinuous, narrow pathways. Most walked barefoot or wore flip-flops. "Gore-Tex®" was not part of their vocabulary.

By the time we reached Manang, six days into the journey, I couldn't get enough of the experience. As the days passed, both Ashley and I felt stronger and stronger. By this time I knew I had chosen the right partner. Although we had set our sights on the summit of Thorong La, I had already reached euphoria seeing Annapurna III rising into the heavens at 24,786 feet. It was too tall, close, imposing, and magnificent to be true.

Everyone who's been to Nepal tells you the Himalayas are big. But nobody had prepared me for the reality of breathing hard at altitudes already near those of some Rocky Mountain peaks, only to see a mountain soar another full height of the Rockies above me. On day nine we reached the high base camp of Thorong Phedi at 14,924 feet. A sign in the hut read, *Richard James Allen died from altitude sickness near the top of Thorong La. 24th Feb 1991—Aged 27 Years. TRAVELERS BEWARE!* Fortunately, we had been warned to spend an extra day to acclimatize at this high elevation.

Namaste.

By the end of Day 10, Ashley and I were as ready as we would ever be. We would attempt to summit the following morning. The night was clear and magnificent as the moon illuminated the jagged white peaks surrounding us. It was the coldest night I have experienced; too cold to stay up, brush my teeth or write in my journal. It would be the first night that my 15F degree North Face Blue Kazoo sleeping bag would not do the trick. With only my nose peeking through my cocoon, I eventually fell asleep with a feeling of excited confidence and pumping adrenaline, as well as an uneasy stomach of nerves.

We started at 5:30 a.m. The sun was not even thinking of appearing yet. Before setting off, Ashley and I threw back a few aspirin as our heads were already pounding from the decreased levels of oxygen. We knew nothing would warm our toes at this point so we didn't even worry about that. An excerpt from my journal reads:

As the mountain became more vertical I felt as if I actually had an overgrown heart hammering in my head as I gasped for more air. At times I lost my balance and felt dizzy. I was only able to take steps where one boot would overlap the other by half. The air is so thin up here that if I start panting even slightly a harsh headache revisits.

The climb would prove to be the most arduous test of stamina I had ever endured. When we finally summited, on top of the world in more ways than one, we embraced and snapped a few photos in a celebration of our achievement.

Atop ThorongLa.

Simultaneously, as the severe effects of oxygen deprivation began to take hold, my brain started to scream that we needed to immediately begin our descent. It was then—and only then—that I realized we still had to navigate the second half of the journey and nightfall was just hours away.

Safe Return(s)

Although arriving at the top of the mountain is considered by many mountaineers to be one of life's greatest accomplishments, I can tell you firsthand that summiting is not the ultimate goal for climbers. They know that 80 percent of climbing accidents and deaths occur on the descent. With this chilling statistic in mind, they will tell you that their objective is to reach the summit and get back down alive to see their family and friends. They understand that the second half of their journey presents the greatest risk and requires the most planning.

The same can be said for the second half of one's financial journey. For years, people have focused intensely on accumulating enough assets (i.e. climbing to the top of the mountain). However the biggest risk facing retirees occurs during the second half of their financial journey, once they retire and begin to live on their retirement savings (i.e. climbing back down the mountain). This is also the phase that requires most of the planning and entails most of the risk. Retirees need to come down the other side safely—no matter what the future brings.

The day you start taking money out of your portfolio and open the income valve to your 401(k) or IRA, all of the rules change. Not only are you no longer adding to your nest egg, you will need to make your money last for a possible 25 to 40 years.

We all know that there are endless books on how to accumulate wealth and how to get out of debt. However, few resources teach what to do once you have reached the top, even though you are faced with unique and potentially devastating risks as you begin the second half of your financial journey. This book was written to fill that gap. Through an unexpected melding of travel and family stories coupled with financial survival tips, *Failure Is Not an Option* will lay out the eight fundamental risks every retiree faces and help you create more certainty in the uncertainty of retirement. In the process, it will help you achieve far greater financial peace of mind, since—just like climbing a mountain—those who recognize and address these risks are most likely to safely and successfully complete their journey.

Chapter 2

FINANCIAL LESSONS FROM
THE MILLIONAIRE NEXT DOOR

You miss 100 percent of the shots you never take.

—Wayne Gretzky

There are people in one's life who act as our guides and impact the fortunes of our lives. My Grandma Ruth, my mother's mother, was one of those. To this day, I continue to pass along the financial principles she instilled in me at an early age.

Born in 1921, Grandma Ruth grew up during the Great Depression. She decided early on that she was never again going to experience the poverty so prevalent in that period. At a time when it was rare for a woman to receive a higher education, she graduated from Brooklyn College with honors. Once my grandfather returned from World War II, she started to learn about investing by joining an investment club with a few friends. Although she was not the income earner of the household, she continuously took 10 percent of my grandfather's paycheck and invested it into the stock market. Although Grandma worked with a few stockbrokers (as there was no such thing as investing on the Internet) and relied on their recommendations, she made the final decisions about when to buy and sell. She felt empowered by investing and incessantly studied the markets. Baseball and football were not Grandma's thing, but the stock market was her game and she became quite knowledgeable about individual stocks, industries and trends in the process.

I will never forget the day she changed the way I thought about money. I was 19 years old. Boys at that age have two things on their minds and cars are one of them. With great enthusiasm, I shared with her the brochure of the brand new Honda Prelude I was going to finance. It was black on black with a stick shift. She knew how to communicate with a teenager, so she stated how proud she was that I was able to purchase a new car at my age (even though the bank would actually be buying it for me).

"You'll have the nicest car of all of your friends," she said, right before she shared with me the chart on the following page and explained what an IRA is, how it benefits investors and how the stock market has performed over the years. She then showed me that if between the ages of 19 and 27 I invested the maximum contribution at the time—$2,000 per year—into an IRA, assuming the account compounded at 10 percent per year I would be a millionaire by age 65 even if I never placed additional contributions into the account. Not only that, but I would have more money than if I started investing $2,000 per year at the age of 27 and did so each and every year until age 65. This is when I truly learned to appreciate what Albert Einstein reportedly considered to be the eighth wonder of the world: the compound interest formula. Grandma taught me the difference between working for money and having money work for me. I never ended up purchasing that car. I started my IRA, a decision that would forever change my life.

THE RETIREMENT BASKET
THE TIME VALUE OF MONEY

	SUSAN investing at age 19 (10% hypothetical annual growth rate)		S E E T H E D I F F E R E N C E	KIM investing at age 27 (10% hypothetical annual growth rate)		
AGE	INVESTMENTS	TOTAL VALUES		AGE	INVESTMENTS	TOTAL VALUES
19	$ 2.000	2.200		19	$ 0	0
20	2.000	4.620		20	0	0
21	2.000	7.282		21	0	0
22	2.000	10.210		22	0	0
23	2.000	13.431		23	0	0
24	2.000	16.974		24	0	0
25	2.000	20.871		25	0	0
26	2.000	25.158		26	0	0
27	0	27.674		27	2.000	2.200
28	0	30.442		28	2.000	4.620
29	0	33.486		29	2.000	7.282
30	0	36.834		30	2.000	10.210
31	0	40.518		31	2.000	13.431
32	0	44.570		32	2.000	16.974
33	0	48.027		33	2.000	20.871
34	0	53.929		34	2.000	25.158
35	0	59.322		35	2.000	29.874
36	0	65.256		36	2.000	35.072
37	0	71.780		37	2.000	40.768
38	0	78.958		38	2.000	47.045
39	0	86.854		39	2.000	53.949
40	0	95.540		40	2.000	61.544
41	0	105.094		41	2.000	69.899
42	0	115.603		42	2.000	79.089
43	0	127.163		43	2.000	89.198
44	0	130.880		44	2.000	100.318
45	0	153.868		45	2.000	112.550
46	0	169.255		46	2.000	126.005
47	0	188.180		47	2.000	140.805
48	0	204.798		48	2.000	157.086
49	0	226.278		49	2.000	174.094
50	0	247.806		50	2.000	194.694
51	0	272.586		51	2.000	216.363
52	0	299.845		52	2.000	240.199
53	0	329.830		53	2.000	266.419
54	0	362.813		54	2.000	295.261
55	0	399.094		55	2.000	326.988
56	0	439.003		56	2.000	361.886
57	0	482.904		57	2.000	400.275
58	0	531.194		58	2.000	442.503
59	0	548.314		59	2.000	488.953
60	0	642.745		60	2.000	540.048
61	0	707.020		61	2.000	596.253
62	0	777.722		62	2.000	658.078
63	0	855.494		63	2.000	726.086
64	0	941.043		64	2.000	800.895
65	0	1.035.148		65	2.000	883.185
Earnings beyond investment: $ 1.019.148				Earnings beyond investment: $ 805.185		

Building a Million Dollar Nest Egg
Ways to Build $ 1.000.000 by age 65 (10% Hypothetical Growth Rate)

Age	Daily Savings	Yearly Savings
20	$ 4.00	$ 1.440
30	$ 11.00	$ 3.960
40	$ 30.00	$ 10.800
50	$ 95.00	$ 34.200

How we live, where we live, what our years of financial independence will look like, are all affected by the success of our finances. Given how important it is to win this game, you would hope to see our schools educating our youth in simple financial basics such as compound interest and the philosophy that how much money one keeps is far more important than how much money one earns. Schools didn't do it then, and they don't do it now. I was lucky enough to have my grandmother to share that lesson with me.

FINANCIAL WISDOM

Grandma was a simple woman. It was not until she passed away that I realized she was in fact the millionaire next door.

Grandma Ruth and me.

The 1996 book *The Millionaire Next Door: The Surprising Secrets of America's Wealthy* is a compilation of research profiling U.S. households having a net worth exceeding one million dollars. The big takeaway for me was that most of the millionaire households they studied did not have the extravagant lifestyles most people would assume. This finding is backed by surveys indicating how little these millionaire households had spent on such things as cars, watches, suits, and other luxury products. Most importantly, the book explains why these people managed to accumulate so much wealth. In summary, they lived well below their means. In fact, the authors make a distinction between the Balance Sheet Affluent (those with actual wealth or high net worth) and the Income Affluent (those with a high income, but little actual wealth or low net worth).

Grandma lived below her means, invested for her future and was able to leave a financial legacy—both in terms of dollars and financial sense. Even as she lay dying in intensive care, the TV above her bed was tuned to the ticker tape of stock prices. She loved the game. I do not believe I would be a financial planner today if it were not for her teaching me what she knew when I was just 19. Today a photo of her hangs proudly in my conference room. As much as I still miss her, I smile every time I look at it.

Grandma taught me to be caring and to enjoy life while living below my means. Her early lessons about how to handle my money and invest it wisely came in handy, since I started working when I was still quite young.

SEAL THE DEAL

It was 1984. I was 15 years of age. Back in those days, home-owners would purchase five-gallon containers of a thick rubbery material to seal coat their driveways. This not only beautified the asphalt, the coating protected it from the damaging effects of repeated freezes and thaws.

I helped my dad seal our driveway and ended up completing the second half of the job on my own. When our next-door neighbor Frank Magavrow saw me sealing our driveway, he asked me if I would do his. The next day my tirelessly supportive mother helped me load five five-gallon containers of sealer from George T. Smith's Hardware Store into the trunk of her Buick Electra. She had no idea what she was getting herself into. Over the next year—until I got my driver's license—her encouragement and willingness to drive me from job to job would help me turn my young dreams of entrepreneurship into a reality. But I'm getting ahead of myself.

I spent much of the day seal coating our neighbor's driveway to perfection and made $25. I was quite excited as my biggest income to that point had been mowing lawns for $5 each. I knew I was on to something. The next day I mimeographed handwritten flyers and dispersed them to every one of the 200 homes in my neighborhood. I ended up sealing eight driveways that summer. The following year, as word of mouth got around (helped by the fact that I placed a handmade sign at every job site), I sealed 25 driveways during my school vacation.

By that point, much to my mother's delight, I had obtained my driver's license. I used my summer profits to purchase my first vehicle—a rusted blue 1972 Chevy pickup truck with a magnetic sign on each door advertising my business. I couldn't have been prouder.

My first driveway sealing pickup truck, 1985.

Business continued to grow significantly during my third season, so I brought on my brother and a few friends to help me. I increased my price to $75 per driveway, a fee commensurate with the rise in the quality of our work. I took the profits and purchased a backpack blower to clean the driveways. I marketed this as a "power pavement cleaner." Then I purchased a John Deere edging machine so we could trim the lawn on the sides of the driveway. That year, we seal coated almost 100 driveways before I headed off to college.

Each summer I would return to grow my business. I started advertising in newspapers. I placed a professional sign (instead of my handcrafted one) in the ground after completing each job. I sent out mass mailers with coupons. Then I decided to emulate my dad.

My father was a successful dentist. I had always admired how he would call each of his patients after a procedure to ask them if they were feeling okay. He also sent out handwritten notes. I began calling all my customers after the job had been completed to ask them if they were satisfied and then followed that up with a thank you note.

I continued to do everything I could to turn a blue-collar business into a white-collar business. My employees and I began calling our customers clients. Our clients did not want the messy, black glop we worked with on their homes, so I started providing a written guarantee stating that if there was a drop of the back sealer on their home, garage doors, sidewalk, lawn, or even on the street, they would get the job for free.

My campaign worked to the point where it became hard to keep up with demand even though I now had four guys working for me. To increase efficiency, I invested in a second vehicle. This time I purchased a van so that we could keep the supplies inside, which I couldn't do with a pickup truck. I continued to raise our prices and we continued to get busier. I let my crew handle the driveway sealing while I drove around providing estimates, checking on our various jobs to make sure they were going well and doing the accounting. We seal coated a couple hundred driveways that summer, prompting our local newspaper to run a front-page story titled "19-Year-Old Entrepreneur Seals His Success." I was making very good money each summer, especially for a college student. Most kids would have focused on what that money could buy them. But thanks to my Grandma, I wasn't most kids.

FINANCIAL FOUNDATION

At the time, one could only place $2,000 per year into an IRA. I wanted to invest more, a desire I shared with my grandmother and my father. They told me about one of the more advantageous retirement accounts of that time—a Money Purchase Pension Plan, which enabled me to invest 25 percent of my income into the plan. I also learned that every dollar I invested for my own financial future was one less dollar I had to pay taxes on. What a deal! I was so excited that I began sharing Grandma's IRA chart with my employees, hoping they would buy into the concepts of paying themselves first and experience the effects of compound interest. Friends and family members started approaching me with investment questions.

By the time I had graduated college, my company was seal coating over 300 driveways per summer. It was time to invest in another vehicle so I went to an auction at the police station and purchased an old, bright yellow paddy wagon. Talk about taking no prisoners! This would enable us to store a lot more product in the vehicle, which we could actually stand up in, and look more professional to boot. I will never forget the day I had my company name plastered in vinyl letters across that wagon.

As summer ended and all my friends had started to send out resumes looking for jobs in the business arena, I decided I would explore the world during the six months that Mother Nature forced me to shut down operations. I told my parents that I would travel for the winter, come home to run the business one more summer and then find a "real job." I decided to head to Fiji, New Zealand, and Australia since they were English-speaking countries, and I had always been intrigued by the nature Down Under. By the following year, however, I still wasn't ready to settle down. Instead, once the weather got cold I turned my focus to Southeast Asia. As you'll see in upcoming chapters, these experiences changed my life—and my perspective about finance—forever.

I ended up seal coating driveways for eight more years. By the time I sold the company at age 30, we were sealing 1,200 driveways a summer and had expanded into power washing decks and siding in order to take advantage of the rainy days when we could not seal coat. By this time my company had added two shiny UPS-style trucks to our small fleet.

During the decade I ran my seal coating business, I managed to spend a month in 65 different countries around the world and meet a New Zealander named Jill who would become my wife. And unlike most 20-somethings, I had already begun to accumulate significant investment savings.

A new fleet of driveway sealing trucks, 1997.

SHARING THE (FINANCIAL) LOVE

I knew my next calling was to help people discover the lessons I had learned from my grandmother and share the knowledge I had acquired from watching my retirement accounts grow. By then I had figured out that people do not need to do anything extraordinary to build wealth for their retirement years. They just need to do some ordinary things (like saving a portion of every paycheck) extraordinarily well (saving a portion of *every* paycheck). By the way, I did not purchase my new car until 11 years after my retirement account had been well established and I had a long-term financial game plan in place.

To this day I know that where I am in life has everything to do with the financial acumen I developed early on thanks to two main sources of inspiration—my father and my grandmother. Grandma needed to teach me how to handle money because I had started to make significant profits at a young age and failure was not an option. This paved the way for my driveway business. My world travels provided lessons that would help me years later when I became a financial planner. Still, neither Grandma nor I could have ever imagined that in the first decade of the new millennium, the impossible would actually become a reality.

Chapter 3

THE IMPOSSIBLE BECOMES A REALITY

Failure is not fatal, but failure to change might be.

—John Wooden

We may not be able to anticipate or even fathom the kind of change that happens around us, but one thing is certain. Those changes—even the ones that seem impossible—happen on a regular basis.

As a teenager in the 1980s, the number one fear for children was the threat of nuclear war. I can remember the drills under our tables at school. Ronald Reagan had just become president and called Russia and their leader Leonid Brezhnev "The Evil Empire." One of my favorite T-shirts stated: *To Russia: The Eagle Is No Chicken.* Beating Russia, no matter the arena, became a national obsession. Then the powerhouse Russian hockey team went up against the U.S. during the 1980 Winter Olympics at Lake Placid, New York, just a short drive from my home.

What a thrill to have the world visit us in our small Adirondack town. That certainly triggered my thirst for world travel. But I will never forget the night that the U.S. hockey team, made up of amateur and collegiate players who had only started playing together months earlier, faced off against the Soviet Union's professional team. The Russians entered the Lake Placid games as the heavy favorite, having won nearly every world championship and Olympic tournament since 1954. I can remember that February day as if it were yesterday. The ABC Sports announcer, Al Michaels screamed, "Do you believe in miracles?" as Team USA beat the Soviets 4-3, eventually going on to secure the gold medal by winning its last match over Finland. The impossible became a reality for this young American team and their "Miracle on Ice" win, dubbed one of the top sports moments of the 20th Century by *Sports Illustrated* almost 20 years later, represented a whole lot more than just a hockey game.

Eight years later, life found me attending a business college in London, England. One day in the middle of a business class filled with international students, a long-bearded German professor barged into the classroom and asked if anyone was interested in joining him for a weeklong educational trip to Berlin, Germany. My new friend John Ambrose from Boston and I looked at each other; without any verbal communication we both lifted our hands high in the air. This sounded like an adventure and certainly more fun than a macro-economics class. Within days we, along with a dozen other students, were on a Lufthansa flight from Heathrow to West Berlin.

THE BERLIN WALL

I had always heard about the Berlin Wall but did not truly know its history. This 12-foot high, 100-mile concrete barricade had been constructed by the German Democratic Republic (East

Germany) in 1961. It completely cut off West Berlin from surrounding East Germany, as well as from East Berlin. This blockade came to symbolize the Iron Curtain that separated Western Europe and the Eastern Bloc during the Cold War. The Eastern Bloc claimed that the wall had been erected to protect its population from fascist elements conspiring to flout the "will of the people." According to them that protection also entailed building a socialist state in East Germany.

A few days after learning about the Berlin Airlift of the late 1940s, which brought food and other needed goods into West Berlin despite a potentially devastating land blockade by East Germany, as well as President Kennedy's celebrated trip to Berlin in 1963 and his famous *Ich bin ein Berliner* speech, we embarked on a day-long sojourn that would change my view of the world we live in. Having procured our obligatory legal documentation, we headed through the legendary crossing point—Checkpoint Charlie. Gone were the bright lights of the progressive and modern west side that embodied capitalism with its Mercedes Benz taxicabs and neon McDonald's signs. Instead, we experienced the gloomy, dilapidated east side of Berlin, with its bullet-scarred buildings and flavorless food that seemed to lack any nourishment.

Looking at the Wall from both sides told a story of two very different societies. The western side was easily accessible, covered in colorful graffiti and poignant messages. In contrast, military patrols, watchdogs and mines secured the eastern side of the Wall. Intimidating guard towers overlooked the "death strip" where throughout the years more than 5,000 people had attempted to escape over, under and through the Berlin Wall. Many of those individuals trying to flee East Germany were shot to death. In all, more than 200 East Germans lost their lives at the Wall, murdered simply because they wished for a different life somewhere else. I remembered when President Reagan had challenged Mikhail Gorbachev to destroy the Berlin Wall the prior year. Standing before the Brandenburg Gate, he thundered, "Tear down this wall!" As I walked along the wall, I certainly didn't anticipate that it would ever come down or that I would be there to witness that in person.

Having caught that infectious condition called the travel bug, the following year I headed off to Istanbul, Turkey—the world's only city located in Europe as well as Asia. This time Eric Johnson, a very close high school friend, accompanied me. We visited prominent attractions including a number of the 3,000 shops in the Grand Bazaar and the historical Blue Mosque. The next day, November 9, 1989, history would be made. The impossible became a reality as the Berlin Wall actually fell. For the first time in almost three decades, citizens from East Germany could visit the west. On storefront televisions, we viewed enormous euphoric crowds celebrating as they chiseled away at the wall with pickaxes. Eric and I looked at each other. We instantly knew that we had to part take in such a historic event. The next morning we boarded a JAT (Air Yugoslavia) jet and headed to the jubilant city of Berlin, the scarce resource of a sledgehammer in hand.

Upon landing in Berlin, we felt like we had joined the world's largest college party. Bars gave out free drinks, strangers kissed and toasted each other with champagne and tearful families reunited. No one had ever seen anything like it. After hours of grueling work with never-ending blows to the four spikes we pounded into the solid wall, we successfully chiseled off a large two-foot section of the wall, which proudly sits today under Lucite on my mantle.

Eric Johnson and me at the Berlin Wall, 1989.

Most of us never imagined the Berlin Wall would come down in our lifetimes. I know I certainly didn't. Its fall would forever change the world in ways we could never have imagined and start a domino effect of capitalism. Twenty years later another supposedly impossible occurrence became a reality and also changed the world in ways we could never have fathomed. This time the collapse involved a financial wall along with many other significant economic foundations.

CRASH!

In 2008, the fate of the world's economy was decided in just a matter of weeks. If someone had told me that the world's largest mortgage company would declare bankruptcy along with the world's largest insurance company, and that the world's largest stock brokerage firm would then fall along with our country's largest investment bank, savings and loan, and automobile company, I would have thought he or she was hallucinating. For crying out loud! And yet today GM is still partially owned by us taxpayers and the Italians own Chrysler.

In short, the impossible became a reality. This is well documented in Andrew Ross Sorkin's bestseller *Too Big to Fail*. I recently had an opportunity to meet Sorkin at a conference he was headlining. He shared that when he wrote his book he was only thinking about financial corporations being too big to fail. He had no idea that just three years later this concept would also pertain to municipalities, states and countries.

Volatility and uncertainty have certainly been recurring themes since 2008. During the same year, the stock market experienced its worst year in history with the S&P 500 Index losing 37 percent. Stocks continued to wrap up their worst January on record in 2009 with an additional 8.6 percent loss. That added up to a 45.5 percent loss in only 13 months. Simultaneously, the U.S. real estate market took a nosedive with the average residence in areas like my home of Bend, Oregon, losing over 50 percent of its value. People were immobilized with fear and if you were at or near retirement, your entire life plan did a 180 right in front of your eyes, losing any profit you had made over the previous ten years.

garyvarvel.com

THE LOST DECADE

The first decade of our millenium is often referred to as the Lost Decade because stocks ended the decade with the same value they had when they started that time span. That happened because the decade experienced not just one recession, but two.

I meet with successful people on a regular basis in my community and around the country who have worked very hard and accomplished much over their lifetime. Many had dreams of retiring early and following their passions with world travel, exciting new hobbies and maybe a cabin on a Cascade or Adirondack lake. After the Lost Decade and the record market volatility we have been experiencing, they are now faced with a new reality.

If your personal expectations about your retirement have changed over the past few years, you're certainly not alone. Today the focus is on managing risk during all of this uncertainty and doing your best to get back on track to the future you envisioned. Retirement is by definition uncertain because the inconceivable often becomes reality. As a result, you start to worry about how to plan for something you can't even fathom, as failure is not an option.

Despite the market's recent rise, retirees still find themselves immobilized by fear as they wonder if they will be able to live the life they had always imagined. Many asked themselves if they should even stay in the market, in the hopes that it would stabilize and rebound to pre-2008 highs or whether they should get out given that stocks could tank even further.

As our country continues to work itself out of the worst economy since the Great Depression and our government teeters due to record budget deficits, I feel it is imperative to examine our relationship with the way we spend, save, borrow, invest and think about money. The days of using our homes as piggy banks to ride the appreciation highway are over. What was typically one's largest asset is often now one's largest liability. It is time to rethink our priorities and get back on track to retirement.

THE UNCERTAINTY OF RETIREMENT

Once upon a time people retired at the age of 65 and received a gold watch after spending many years working diligently for the same company. They had a reasonable expectation that they could live out their remaining 12 to 15 years comfortably, thanks to their pension, Social Security and a steady flow of dividends and interest from safe, conservative stocks and bonds. No more! What has changed? In the past Social Security was considered a sure thing. Today we face potential cutbacks and many call our government allowance Social Insecurity. What was intended as a safety net has morphed into an entitlement program.

The very foundation of the Social Security system is cracked. This crack will not disappear, but will only grow larger and more dangerous. If any company were operating on the same basis as the current Social Security program, it would have been put out of business years ago. The fundamental problem lies in the fact that when Social Security was started in 1935, it was intended to provide only a supplemental retirement income source to a minority of Americans. Today, as we are retiring earlier and living longer, it has instead become the primary retirement income source for a majority of retired Americans. Social Security provides at least half of the retirement income for two out of every three Americans. Those aged 85 and older receive 80 percent of their income from Social Security.

Some 56 million people collect Social Security benefits, and that is projected to grow to 91 million in 2035. In 1950, 16.5 people in the work force funded the system for every benefactor. Today fewer than three people fund every benefactor.

The Social Security Administration estimates its shortfall at $8.6 trillion. That means the agency would need to invest $8.6 trillion today, and have that investment pay returns of 2.9 percent above inflation for the next 75 years to produce enough money to cover the shortfall.

The system is truly overburdened and running out. The next time you receive your social security statement in the mail, take the time to read the fine print on the front page. Until recently, the form stated:

In 2017 we will begin paying more in benefits than we collect in taxes. Without changes, by 2041 the Social Security Trust Fund will be exhausted.

Now it reads:

Without changes, in 2033 the Social Security Trust Fund will be able to pay only about 77 cents for each dollar of scheduled benefits.

Prevent identity theft—protect your Social Security number

Your Social Security Statement

www.socialsecurity.gov

Prepared especially for Wanda Worker

May 31, 2013

See inside for your personal information ➡

WANDA WORKER
456 ANYWHERE AVENUE
MAINTOWN, USA 11111-1111

What's inside...

Your Estimated Benefits...2
Your Earnings Record...3
Some Facts About Social Security...............................4
If You Need More Information.....................................4

What Social Security Means To You

This *Social Security Statement* can help you plan for your financial future. It provides estimates of your Social Security benefits under current law and updates your latest reported earnings.

Please read this *Statement* carefully. If you see a mistake, please let us know. That's important because your benefits will be based on our record of your lifetime earnings. We recommend you keep a copy of your *Statement* with your financial records.

Social Security is for people of all ages. We're more than a retirement program. Social Security also can provide benefits for disabled and help support

Work to build a secure future. Social Security is the largest source of income for most elderly Americans today, but Social Security was never intended to be your only source of income when you retire. You also will need other savings, investments, pensions or retirement accounts to make sure you have enough money to live comfortably when you retire.

Saving and investing wisely are important not only for you and your family, but for the entire country. If you want to learn more about how and why to save, you should visit *www.mymoney.gov*, a federal government website dedicated to teaching all Americans the basics of financial management.

About Social Security's future... Social Security is a compact between generations. Since 1935, America has kept the promise of

security for its workers and their families. Now, however, the Social Security system is facing serious financial problems, and action is needed soon to make sure the system will be sound when today's younger workers are ready for retirement.

Without changes, in 2033 the Social Security Trust Fund will be able to pay only about 77 cents for each dollar of scheduled benefits.* We need to make sure Social Security continues...

"Without changes, in 2033 the Social Security Trust Fund will be able to pay only about 77 cents for each dollar of scheduled benefits."

Carolyn W. Colvin
Acting Commissioner

* These estimates are based on the intermediate assumptions from the Social Security Trustees' Annual Report to the Congress.

Clearly, not even the government is sure about how Social Security is faring. Indeed, both statements could be correct. Either way, the conclusions point to a shortfall should Congress not be able to agree on how to overhaul the program. "We need to resolve these issues soon to make sure Social Security continues to provide a foundation of protection for future generations," concludes Social Security's Acting

Commissioner Carolyn W. Colvin. Of course, we've all seen Congress dismal record when it comes to bi-partisan action.

The simple conclusion you might want to draw?

Social Security is not as robust as it once was and can no longer be counted on as a given when calculating your retirement income.

That's just the start when it comes to financial insecurity during your retirement years. Many companies have replaced defined benefit pension plans with defined contribution plans that do not offer the same degree of assured income. Pension plans have been phased out and the shift from traditional pensions to 401(k)s has made retirement a riskier prospect because retirees must now manage their investments and control spending on their own.

Retirees were certainly startled in 2008 when they witnessed their holdings inside their retirement accounts plummet. Fortunately the markets have experienced significant growth since then and have even hit new records, but now bond yields have hit rock bottom and CDs are only offering negligible returns. With an estimated 10,000 people retiring a day, it's no wonder that the primary concern among many retirees is simply making ends meet.

I recently created a comprehensive financial blueprint for a client who had just retired after working as an international businessman for 34 years at Kodak. In 1976, the Eastman Kodak Company, which was founded in 1889, had a 90 percent market share of photographic film sales in the United

States. The company's tagline—*Kodak moment*—entered the common vocabulary to describe a personal event that demanded to be recorded for posterity. My client started with Kodak right about at that peak period. Shortly after he had retired, our projections showed that between his $48,000 annual pension from Kodak, his social security and his other investments, he and his wife were financially independent and had a very high probability of never outliving their income. Just weeks after completing the couple's plan, Kodak declared bankruptcy and my client informed me in a disheartened tone of disbelief that he had been told not to expect a dime of his pension. This was not the Kodak moment he and his wife had in mind and they were no longer singing Paul Simon's hit song "Kodachrome." The impossible had become a reality for this once Dow 30 Company as well as for my client and his spouse, who now have to restructure their entire financial future in retirement.

A JUGGLING ACT

We used to say that baby boomers were the "Sandwich Generation," caught between trying to save enough money to get the kids through college while taking care of their elderly parents financially. That sandwich generation has turned into the triple-decker "Club Sandwich Generation," because in addition to the fiscal challenges involving kids and parents, they also have to worry about staying afloat and funding their *own* retirements.

Although many indicators show that the economy is improving around the country, national studies paint a discouraging picture revealing that amid low savings rates, high unemployment and declining wealth, a majority of Americans run the risk of running out of money in retirement. Add in saving for a child's college education, and you truly have a dilemma. Most hard-working families today simply can't afford to financially prepare for their own retirement. And they certainly can't afford to finance their kids' schooling. Knowing how challenging this is for their families, many of my retired clients have expressed a strong desire to invest for their grandchildren's college educations. I love that idea, as long as they have the means to do so without financially jeopardizing themselves. I have always been one to stress the importance of education. I don't ask my children if they are going to college. I ask them where they would like to go to college. With that being said, I typically suggest to most families that they put retirement first.

A new Millionaire Corner survey shows that investors are seven times more likely to identify *adequate retirement savings*—as opposed to *college tuition*—as their most significant financial concern. In fact, retirement savings trumps the entire menu of financial worries, including job security, personal debt, home values, inflation and health care costs, while college tuition comes in dead last. Only 4 percent of investors identify college costs as their top financial concern, compared to nearly 28 percent who say they are most worried about saving enough money to last through retirement.

That makes a lot of sense if we use the airplane analogy: In the event of a sudden drop in cabin pressure, put on your own oxygen mask first, and then help children who are traveling with you. The example serves to illustrate the importance of helping yourself first, so that you'll be in a better position to help others. Parents who make saving for college tuition a priority may run the risk of running short of funds in retirement and becoming a burden on others.

Now What?

To say we are currently facing a great deal of economic uncertainty is undoubtedly an understatement even if you don't have to worry about supporting parents or underwriting children's college tuition. With so much now out of our control, it is all too common today to meet people who despite having accumulated significant wealth still have grave concerns about how uncertain their financial future seems to be.

Much of the talk on Wall Street as well as what we read in the media tends to focus on the current challenges, negative statistics and high emotions we are experiencing. But this doesn't have to be the end of the world. My intention is not to sugarcoat reality or pretend that our current situation is not as serious as it is. I am aware that many of us are currently facing troublesome times. But I feel we can all benefit by facing our present circumstances with as little emotion—and as much information—as possible about the strategies that can help mitigate the financial risks we run.

How do you shift your mindset, especially when you became so accustomed to record economic growth in previous years? Whether you are at or near retirement, you must plan for financial independence now more than ever before.

Chapter 4

IF YOU FAIL TO PLAN,
YOU ARE PLANNING TO FAIL

You who are on the road
must have a code that you can live by.

—*Graham Nash*

There is an old saying: "If you fail to plan, you are planning to fail." As you'll soon see, this was certainly relevant during my sojourn through Australia's Outback, because when you're out in the middle of nowhere, failure is not an option.

I arrived in Sydney, Australia, with the mindset that a drive across the Outback might just be the best road trip available on this planet. I visited the Saturday Car Market and hours later was the proud owner of a 1972 Holden Kingswood station wagon which would provide the means for my exploration of the vast and inauspicious region as well as shelter when necessary. My plan was to drive from Sydney down to Melbourne, over to Adelaide, up to Alice Springs—the heart of the Outback—then to Cairns and back down to Sydney. My journey would be similar to driving from North Carolina over to Texas, up to Nebraska, over to Maine and back down the east coast to North Carolina. The one big difference is that driving in Australia, especially in the Outback, gives distances an altered meaning.

Upon arriving in Adelaide a couple of weeks later, I had the good fortune to meet Ross Armstrong. Ross was an Englishman about my age with the same goal of experiencing the Australian Outback. It did not take long for me to realize that with his English humor, sense of adventure and our having so much in common, we would make good travel companions. He agreed, and we decided we would set off for this exploit of a lifetime together.

We were warned that if you are driving in the Outback you must be prepared for anything, but what exactly did "anything" mean? It turns out that motorists may travel for hundreds of miles between towns or roadhouses without opportunities to refuel, get water, obtain supplies, or use toilets. We clearly needed to be self-sufficient and prepared for emergencies. There would be limited traffic should we break down, so a substantial amount of time might elapse before anyone will pass. In addition, the interior of Australia is a true desert with daytime temperatures commonly ranging from 113°F to 122°F on really hot days and nighttime temperatures potentially dropping to freezing. This can be a serious problem for the unprepared. We could have really gotten into trouble since my recently purchased station wagon did not have an air conditioner, but at least the heater worked.

Lessons From Down Under

As Ross and I prepared for our journey, we took a number of important recommendations to heart:

- If at all possible, don't go it alone. The best way to avoid trouble is to find some other vehicle to accompany you on your drive. We were not successful in this, but we did find two other passengers who would defray some of our costs and add to the fun.
- Be aware of fuel supplies and always allow a generous reserve for unexpected contingencies. Distances between gas stations can be extreme, even on main roads, and conditions can change without warning. A good rule of thumb is to carry sufficient fuel to be able to turn around and return to the place you were last able to secure adequate provisions. We brought three five-gallon containers of additional fuel.
- Take at least ten liters of drinking water per person per day of travel, and an additional three to five days of extra drinking water per person in case of breakdown. We brought a five-gallon water container per person.
- Bring a few extra days' worth of food as well as a camp stove.
- Have two to three spare tires. The faster you drive, the bigger your chance to have one of your tires split open from sharp-edged rocks on the road. We purchased three additional tires.
- Bring extra engine oil (we brought two gallons), fan belts, spare keys, clear plastic in case something happens to the windshield and a tool box.
- Have your vehicle undergo comprehensive service before you leave. If your vehicle suffers a breakdown, remain close to the vehicle. Don't set out for help unless you definitely know where you're going and that you can get there.
- Watch out for animals. Wildlife is plentiful in the Outback, and kangaroos, emus, wombats, horses and rabbits as well as cattle frequently wander onto roadways.

Enormous red kangaroos in particular will leap across the roadways directly in front of vehicles. Most animal collisions occur at dusk, at dawn, or at night when many animals are both more active and less visible.

• Once you are outside the metropolitan areas, traffic tends to thin out and driving becomes relatively boring. The long, straight stretches and hot temperatures can be a recipe for drowsiness. Make sure you stop every couple of hours to change drivers. People die on these roads from drivers falling asleep.

• Road trains are a special hazard on Australian roads. These monsters can reach lengths of up to 150 feet, with up to four trailers hitched behind one truck. Oncoming road trains should be given all the space they need. If possible, slow down and drive partly on the shoulder. A road train coming up behind you should be allowed to pass, but be aware that when they overtake you at high speeds, they can create a vortex that sucks you toward them. Therefore be alert and stay in control of your vehicle at all times.

After a few chockfull days of preparation, the wagon was fully stocked, serviced and ready for our unforgettable escapade. Feeling both excited and apprehensive, Ross and I took off with our new English friends, Helen and Tracey, who were looking for a ride to Cairns and were willing to share in the driving and expenses. We took off for the Stuart Highway, which runs from south to north through the center of the continent. Little did we know at the time what was in store for us and how valuable the advice listed above would prove.

Australians drive on the left side of the road and have the steering wheel on their right side. This took some getting used to as the indicator (turn signal) stalk is on the right side of the steering wheel and the windshield wiper stalk is on the left side of the steering wheel. Any time I wanted to indicate an upcoming turn, I would inadvertently turn on the wipers. I learned early on not to tell the Aussies (Australians) that they drive on the *wrong* side of the road but rather to state that we drive on the *other* side of the road.

In the Outback with my new Holden wagon and friends from England.

After ten hours of driving, we spent our first night close to the site where the movie "Mad Max" was filmed, in the town of Coober Pedy, a name that comes from the Aboriginal term kupa-piti, which means "white man's hole." The town with a population of about 1,500 is sometimes referred to as the opal capital of the world because of the quantity of precious opals

mined there. Due to the scorching daytime heat, Coober
Pedy is known for its belowground residences, called dug-
outs. That evening we slept in an underground hostel, our
rooms chiseled from the earth and full of bunk beds. The
next morning we stopped at the petrol station before heading north into a dry sea of nothingness. We had learned the
previous day that the engine required almost two liters of oil
every three hundred miles. I asked the gas attendant, "Please
check the gas and fill up the oil."

After a few hours of driving, I let Helen take the wheel. By this
time we were all in our own zone, listening to music, writing in
our journals or taking a nap. Mesmerized by the heat and the
endless road, Helen closed her eyes for just a moment and actually fell asleep at the wheel. Suddenly, the car made an abrupt
90-degree, left-hand turn. We bounced off the edge of the road
and careened onto the arid terrain that thankfully stretched for
miles. Every time we hit a rock, the car jolted, adding to what
can only be described as our frenetic sense of panic. Had we
not been belted in, our heads would have hit the top of the car
as well as the side windows. After what seemed like an extended period of time but was probably a matter of ten seconds or
less, Helen managed to bring the car to a stop. Shaken, we all
piled out to take a breather. Helen was on the verge of tears.
"I could have killed everyone," she exclaimed, her voice shaky.

We decided to give the car a chance to cool down, and Helen
a chance to recover, before driving onward. That evening we
found a small campground. The girls set up their tent as Ross
and I slept in the car for the first time. A foam mattress made
for a comfortable evening as the temperatures cooled off con-
siderably. Seeing the Southern Cross for the first time in the

brilliant sky of the Southern Hemisphere was a sight I will never forget. In that blissful moment, I couldn't help but sing the Crosby Stills and Nash song by the same name.

The next day was a scorcher with temperatures approaching 120°F. I had never experienced such heat. Just two hours into our drive a tire blew. With the extreme temperatures exacerbated by the asphalt's absorption of the heat and the friction of the tread on the road, the rubber actually melted. We emptied much of the wagon's contents to dig out one of the three spares. Thirty minutes later, we were off once again. We got a whole hour down the road before another tire blew! Ross and I now worked like a NASCAR squad when it came to changing tires in a jiffy, but this time we experienced the worst flies ever. They were as big as horse flies and they were everywhere. We would later find out that locals dangle corks from the brims of their hats to keep these menacing insects out of their mouths. Our solution was to wrap our heads in our T-shirts.

By mid afternoon we had entered the state of Queensland. The landscape changed to grasslands and the quality of the roads deteriorated significantly. Now we had to contend with potholes and crumbling shoulders. The road was only a lane and a half wide, so every time another vehicle approached someone had to pull over. When we encountered a 50-meter road train, there was absolutely no doubt who was boss. The driver thundered by our stopped car at about 80 miles an hour, showering our windscreen with rocks from the shoulder of the road. Older Australian cars do not have laminated windshields so glass shattered all over us in uncountable fragments. As startled as we were, we felt fortunate to be unhurt.

We had brought along a clear plastic sheet in case of just such an incident, but that lasted only a few miles before tearing. Every time another vehicle approached, we pulled completely over in fear of rocks being flung into the car. By the time the sun had set, all eight eyes straining to see lurking cattle and kangaroos, we felt unquestionably deflated. Suddenly biblical proportions of locusts appeared. Swarms of these grasshopper-like insects assaulted us from every angle. Hundreds entered our car due to the lack of a windshield, many dying on impact as they painfully bashed into our bodies. The fortunate ones began jumping all over the car. If this was not enough, the locusts wound up clogging the radiator, causing the car to overheat. We scraped off the locusts glued to the front of the car and with a dejected feeling of defeat eventually drove at a snail's pace in the dark to the town of Mount Isa, 110 miles away.

The broken windshield after a road train passed by.

Can you imagine what our outcome would have been had we not planned appropriately for this journey? Two decades later, Ross and I remain very dear friends. We get together a couple of times each year and relive our Outback adventure. Each time we acknowledge and give thanks for the preparation we had in place.

Preparation is every bit as vital when it comes to planning your financial journey. One does not become independent of a paycheck by accident. Unfortunately when it comes to Americans retiring, only a small percentage of people are able to maintain the same standard of living they experienced during their working years. This is a tragic statistic especially when we consider that Americans work more hours than any other nation in the world—including Japan. Even after working a majority of their lives, most Americans are unable to achieve financial independence. They clearly need to review a few baseball basics.

SPRING TRAINING TIPS

You may have heard the tale of the New York cabbie who answers a tourist's question about how to get to Carnegie Hall: "Practice, practice, practice." This reminds me of major league baseball players—seasoned athletes who have committed their lives to their sport. These guys have been playing this American pastime since they were toddlers. They are the very best baseball players in the world. And yet what do they do every year at Spring Training? They practice hitting, they practice catching, and they practice throwing. World-class athletes— along with all the rest who strive to be the best in their fields of endeavor—drill for skill obsessively. They practice, practice,

practice. They make sure they're as prepared as they can possibly be when it is game time.

These lessons carry over from the ballpark to planning for your financial future. Why aren't more people showing up for the financial equivalent of spring training? Sadly, I believe most people spend more time planning their vacation each year than they do planning their financial future.

Many successful people thought they were properly prepared to weather the undulations of the stock and real estate markets, and yet when the "Perfect Retirement Storm" rolled in with devastating force, most were truly not equipped, organized or ready. As a result, a lot of folks in their 50s and 60s will need to continue working longer than they had planned. We all know people at or near retirement who had to either delay their departure date from work or re-enter the workforce.

If you're like most, even if you are already financially independent and are defining your golden years through other activities, you probably have concerns about your financial future. Considering the unprecedented times of uncertainty we live in, that trepidation is absolutely understandable.

When the last financial crisis hit, many investors were devastated by crushing blows to their retirement accounts. Exhausted and emotionally frustrated, many became immobilized and did nothing. Some are still doing nothing. But burying your head in the sand doesn't help you avoid the dust storm. Instead, it all but guarantees you'll get blown away or buried.

You may find yourself extremely unsettled by the ups and downs of the market. To make matters worse, it has become increasingly difficult to make educated decisions about what you should do with your money. From television to next-door neighbors to Internet chat rooms, everyone seems to have an opinion. But how can you be sure you are getting the right advice? What can you do to ensure you make the right choices?

IN SHORT, WHAT'S A PERSON TO DO?

I have a four-word answer to the above questions: *Get the right help.*

A secure retirement is not an accident—it is the result of planning. Markets go up and markets go down, but good planning can help you take control of your finances. To build a successful retirement plan, you need to devote time to do your homework or seek the assistance of a financial professional— someone who can help guide key decisions. A comprehensive financial plan can help you negotiate the twists and turns of the market because your investment strategy is based on *your* own situation and goals—not what the market is doing at the moment. Today retirement planning should involve more than investment decisions. It should look at all the moving pieces of your financial picture.

I find that many successful people have been very focused on their careers, but lack a clear vision of what they would like their retirement years to look like. Before having a true plan in place many had visions of freedom and folly that were often interrupted with anxiety and doubt. *Can*

I even afford to retire at all? Will I be able to sustain my lifestyle? Why didn't I do more? Is it too late? How will I recover from the losses my stock and real estate portfolios have experienced?

If you're like most people, you know that you can live comfortably at the start of your retirement, but you're probably less sure about whether you'll have the resources to maintain your lifestyle 10, 20 and 30 years down the road. Planning and preparation make all the difference in the quality of your retirement years. It's not luck that enables people to retire, travel, and enjoy themselves. It is planning that develops strategies to overcome the eight key risks of retirement we'll be discussing in the next two chapters.

The motto *If we take a late retirement and an early death, we'll just squeak by* is not a prudent one. Historically the fear of public speaking, which I used to call public sweating, was considered the number one fear in America, followed by the fear of death. Snakes, spiders and heights are all it takes to send many people cowering in the corner. However with over 10,000 baby boomers retiring each day, I believe the fear of outliving one's retirement income has become one of the most significant fears in America. The real-life genesis of this well-founded fear must be stopped.

In your personal finance world, you can emulate champion athletes by setting realistic goals and committing to them. You can follow the champs' example by working with a seasoned coach committed to your success. You can use the best equipment. You can track your statistics, review the progress you're making toward your goals, and adjust your game plan to stay on course. Practice and preparation are the lessons we can borrow from professional athletes.

So the next time you watch a major league baseball game, think about your own game plan for financial success and make sure you get on the ball. As I discovered in the Australian Outback, survival depends on not going it alone and enlisting the right people you can depend on. In the world of financial advising, that means going with an independent.

THE BENEFITS OF GOING INDEPENDENT

What advantages does an independent financial advisor offer? Unlike an in-house advisor who is limited to the menu of products approved by his employer, independent financial advisors can help investors make informed and objective investment choices from a wide range of financial products. An independent advisor has a single fiduciary responsibility. He is beholden only to you rather than to an investment or insurance company. Historically, various brokerage firms have manufactured products and incentivized their sales force to sell those specific products. For example, if a retired couple is looking to invest a portion of their portfolio into an annuity and they're working with even a top-notch agent from a specific insurance company, that agent typically can only share his or her company's product. No matter how good that company may be there is no single product that is the most advantageous for all people in all circumstances. Compare that to an independent advisor who helps you determine your needs, researches all of the viable options and then shares with you the one or two he or she deems to be the most appropriate and beneficial for your specific needs. Even though independent advisors have no ties to Wall Street firms, they can offer virtually all of top-rated financial products available today at the same price you'd pay anywhere else.

In my experience, preeminent advisors do everything possible to ensure that their goals align with their clients', removing as much of the sales process as possible from the equation. Here's how top financial advisors accomplish this:

- They charge for their expertise. How much do most financial advisors charge for their advice? The answer is nothing! Zero! Nada! Can you imagine this being the case with your attorney or CPA? These financial advisors only get compensated when they sell you an investment or insurance product. Is this in your best interest? Of course not. As consumers we love to buy, but we have an aversion to being sold. I enjoy buying a new car, but the thought of entering a showroom and having a salesman try and sell me a car is not a comfortable thought. Successful families who take their finances seriously prefer to pay for advice rather than be sold financial products that may not be the best fit for them.
- They guarantee your satisfaction. Once the financial planning process is complete, they refund 100 percent of the planning fee if the client does not feel their expectations regarding the value they got out of the plan have been met or surpassed.
- They pledge to never discuss specific investment or insurance strategies until the plan has been returned, accepted, a strong level of trust has developed between the advisor and the client, and the client has *invited* the advisor to share different viable options.

- They have access to the vast majority of A+-rated investment and insurance companies from around the globe. And since they do not represent a specific investment or insurance company, their only responsibility is to YOU.

These top advisors share how they are compensated without having to be asked. Independent advisors do not work on commission where they receive a large payout up front and no continual income in the future. When working with commissioned financial advisors, clients often wonder why the stellar service they received in the beginning dwindles to the point where it becomes a challenge to get their advisor to even return a phone call. Compensation tends to breed behavior. It is in everyone's best interest when an advisor has to continually earn his or her client's business. By charging an annual fee, billed quarterly, based on the assets the advisor manages, both parties are on the same side of the fence. They want the accounts to increase appropriately over time. When the markets increase, the advisor charges a percentage of a larger portfolio. When the markets decline, which they inevitably will in certain years, the advisor charges that same percentage of a smaller portfolio. So it's in his or her interest to make sure that your accounts grow appropriately over time.

BEING PREPARED

A truly independent financial advisor represents you and not a Wall Street firm, which can make all the difference. As you transition from the wealth accumulation phase to the wealth distribution phase of your life, however, it is important to realize that there is no magic solution, no one way to achieve financial success. Having an objective and independent plan in place *can* help you create greater certainty around the uncertainty of retirement. The hoped-for reward for all this planning is living the life you have always imagined during your years of financial independence and of course having peace of mind.

Throughout your journey into retirement, you'll run a gauntlet of risks even more daunting than those I faced in Australia. As I discovered on my journey through the Outback, knowing what those are allows you to prepare for them. And that will help determine whether your journey is a successful one or not.

Chapter 5

THE RISKS OF LIVING AND LIVING WELL

The bad news is time flies. The good news is you're the pilot.

—Michael Altshuler

Before embarking on a journey it is important to understand the guidelines for a safe and successful experience. The same is true when planning for retirement because (repeat after me) failure is not an option. In your years of retirement there are no mulligans or second chances. The day you turn on the spigot to your 401(k) or IRA, all of the rules change. Instead of contributing to your pool of funds, you'll be taking funds out. Over the next 20 to 40 years, you will be dependent on this income stream you've spent a lifetime accumulating. I refer to this period as the Fragile Risk Zone.

The good news is that instead of contributing to your retirement fund, you're finally going to start benefitting from distributions. The bad news is that you must understand and overcome serious risks that were not nearly as significant during the accumulation phase of your working years. Creating a RISK (Retirement Income Survival Kit) Blueprint™ will help to ensure that your money lasts as long as (or longer than) you do. In short, you need to ensure that your income streams are protected against the eight key retirement risks that you, and indeed all retirees, face.

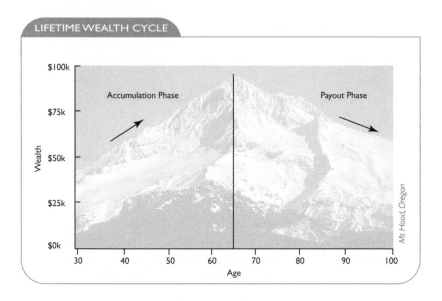

LIFETIME WEALTH CYCLE

Addressing Retirement RISK #1: INFLATION RISK

The first—and some would say most threatening—risk to financial independence is inflation. Oddly enough, I learned about how much risk inflation poses in Vietnam.

In 1993, 18 years after the Vietnam War ended and the country became communist, I spent five weeks traveling by bus, train, and thumb from Saigon to Vietnam's capital city of Hanoi located 700 miles to the north. I visited the Cu Chi Tunnels, a sprawling underground network of tunnels that secretly housed thousands of Viet Cong (VC) fighters during the war,

Hamburger Hill, Monkey Mountain near Da Nang, China Beach, and perhaps the most infamous site in all of Vietnam, the Hanoi Hilton (Hoa Lo Prison) where American POWs including Senator John McCain were jailed and tortured.

Ever since a number of my friends' fathers returned from the war that left them so traumatized that they would never discuss it, I've always reached out to shake the hand of any Vietnam veteran I've met. I look into their eyes and I sincerely thank them for their service. Maybe that's why no place impacted me more than Khe Sanh. This base was home to 6,000 U.S. Marines and 5,000 airplanes and helicopters. The area was once surrounded by dense jungle; today the land is barren with only green grass returning to the undulating hills. The U.S. forces used Agent Orange to disintegrate every living organism in the region, thereby rendering the Viet Cong more easily detectable. As I looked around, I could barely conceive that 500 American and 10,000 North Vietnamese soldiers lost their lives there.

I wasn't supposed to be in Vietnam, but I was too intrigued not to go. President Clinton had not yet signed the U.S.-Vietnam Bilateral Trade Agreement, so the U.S. trade embargo was still in place. Americans were not even permitted to enter the country as visiting was considered trading. So I was very nervous landing at Tân Sơn Nhất International Airport. How would the South Vietnamese react to an American considering that we had left them to face years of oppression from their northern countrymen? With more than a little anxiety, I explained to the customs officer that he could not stamp my passport. He understood and respectfully stamped a piece of paper instead, which he placed into my passport.

I had unofficially entered the Socialist Republic of Vietnam. People in the airport stared at me but no one seemed to be bothered by the only westerner in sight. Before I could even figure out how to find a bus or taxi to get to the city center, a handful of eager Korean men approached me. In broken English, they asked if they could hire me to be filmed in their motion picture documenting the Vietnam War for the South Korean market. I was an easy target as there weren't too many westerners traveling to Vietnam at that time. They offered to pay me $25 to play the part of Lieutenant Gary B. Parker. This remains one of the most surreal experiences of my life. Within hours of fearfully walking off the plane, I was dressed in an American lieutenant's uniform, standing outside the Rex Hotel on the streets of downtown Saigon. This icon was made famous during the Vietnam War when its rooftop bar became a well-known hangout spot for military officials and war correspondents.

Playing the role of Lieutenant Gary B. Parker.

From the other side of the roped-off street, large crowds watched the filming. They were all very interested in me, wondering if I was a famous Hollywood actor or an American officer. Either way, they wanted an autograph. The shoot went well into the night. I had no lines, but rode in a horse and buggy for endless takes as I drank Tiger Beer and used up five of my fifteen minutes of fame. I couldn't imagine a more attention-grabbing introduction to Vietnam until the next morning when I acquired a visceral sense of what inflation truly means.

My favorite part of being in Vietnam was interacting with the children, most of whom had never seen a westerner.

The first thing I usually do upon entering a new country, besides starring in a motion picture, is to exchange money into the local currency. In 1993 there were no ATM machines in Vietnam so I carried Travelers Checks in my money belt which, hidden under my clothes, rested tightly around my waist. When I gave the bank teller $100, I received 2,083,333 Vietnamese dong. The largest denomination they had at the time was a 1,000 dong bill, so I left the bank with a grocery bag overflowing with over 2,000 bills. My facial expression must have revealed how uneasy I felt. *How will I get back to my hotel with all of this money? Is this dangerous? Where will I put it once I get there?*

Trying to stuff bills in my money belt.

The inflation rate in Vietnam that year was 37.7 percent. Although this may sound ludicrous, it is well below the 200 percent inflation rate the country had experienced a decade earlier in 1982. To put this in perspective, the United States has historically experienced an average annual inflation rate between 3 percent and 4 percent. Although inflation jumped as high as 13.5 percent in 1980, we have also experienced deflation, which occurs when the inflation rate falls below 0 percent as it did in 2009. By 1994 in Vietnam, 100,000 dong notes had been introduced in response to the incredible and sustained rates of inflation.

During the second half of your financial journey, it is critical that you be able to maintain your purchasing power. Simply put, inflation means that every year your money buys a little—or a lot—less than it did the year before. The current inflation rate of 3.5 percent may not sound like much, especially when we compare it to countries like Vietnam. But even this rate of inflation means that prices will double every 20 years. How does this impact your retirement?

Inflation erodes your purchasing power. Let's take a look at inflation's detrimental effects during a 30-plus year retirement. In 1980 the average new car cost $7,574. Today that same car costs over $30,000. In 1980 the average new home cost $62,900. Today the average cost of a new home is over $300,000.

Imagine retiring at age 60 with an annual income of $100,000. Twenty years later at the age of 80, you will need to withdraw $200,000 from your same retirement accounts just to maintain that same standard of living. This doesn't even factor in additional costs of health care and possible long-term care expenses. If you happen to live to age 100, this figure will have doubled once again and you will need $400,000 each year to purchase what $100,000 purchases today. When clients find this hard to fathom, I share with them that they probably spent more money on their last automobile than their parents spent purchasing their first home. This is when they begin to see the daunting effects of inflation. Then I share with them that it is highly likely we are going to be entering an inflationary period as the Fed prints more bills and interest rates eventually rise, thereby triggering a related rise in the inflation rate. I don't want to scare them, but they need to understand how down the line inflation can impact their bottom line by devaluing how much their money is actually worth.

One of my favorite television shows from childhood was "Gilligan's Island," the story of seven castaways deserted on a beautiful tropical island. Recently my wife and I introduced our kids to this goofy and upbeat show through Netflix. It is a joy to see them giggle incessantly to the silliness of Gilligan. His companions the Skipper, the Hollywood actress and the professor all bring back so many fun memories along with a sense of youthful innocence. Perhaps the most inspiring characters were "the millionaire and his wife," Thurston Howell, III and Mrs. "Lovey" Howell. They lived in a Beverly Hills mansion, traveled the world and owned every material possession imaginable. I still find it perplexing how they fit most of it on the Minnow for their three-hour tour.

As millionaires they were accustomed to being waited on hand and foot. They seemed to not have any worries in their lives. Being a millionaire in the 1960s was something we could all dream of as it meant a lifestyle of complete luxury. Less than half a century later the concept of being a millionaire has dramatically changed. Although one should feel blessed to have a million dollars since most people in the United States and certainly around the world will never experience such wealth, have they really hit the big time like the Howells?

While $1 million was once a sign that you had arrived, plenty of people with up to $10 million today don't think of themselves as rich. Many actually consider themselves middle class, according to survey work by the authors of the book *The Middle-Class Millionaire*. A few years ago, Barron's published an article referring to families with under $25 million of net worth as "beer and pretzel" millionaires. Although most people would be delighted to be a middle-class millionaire, the lesson here is that as you plan your years of financial independence it is essential to have an investment game plan in place that will accommodate the damaging effects of inflation, especially since we're all living longer and longer.

Addressing Retirement Risk #2: LONGEVITY

Americans are not only living longer, they're retiring earlier. I refer to this growing gap as the Age Wave. During the last century, our life expectancy has almost doubled. Not only are people living longer, the proportion of our older population in this country is also rising dramatically. Think about this: The U.S. Census Bureau states that the over-80 population is increasing five times faster than the overall population. By 2030, the demographics of 32 states will resemble those of Florida today.

Not only do more years of retirement now need to be financed, graying now means playing! Rocking chairs aren't for today's grandparents. Retirement will likely involve more planes, trains and automobiles as well as skis, stand-up paddleboards and golf clubs. According to the Congressional Budget Office, only about half of all those baby boomers will have enough to maintain their standard of living throughout retirement. It's not luck that enables people to retire younger, travel, and enjoy themselves forever more; it's planning. As we have discussed, relying on Social Security or a company pension used to be enough, but today your own retirement savings have become an increasingly important factor in how comfortable you will be in retirement.

As life expectancy grows, will you and millions of baby boomers have enough to live on? According to *SmartMoney*, the average length of retirement increased from 8.1 years in 1950 to more than 20 years in 2012. Americans are retiring younger and living longer. According the National Center for Health Statistics, by the year 2050 about one million Americans will be at least 100 years old. Consider Jeanne Calment who entered the Guinness Book of World Records when she passed away in 1997 at the age of 122. Consider that last year Hallmark Cards Inc. sold 85,000 100th birthday cards.

I recently visited my beloved Great Aunt Lila and Great Uncle Marvin, the latter who sadly passed away shortly before the publication of this book. At the time, they resided at a pleasant assisted-living facility in Florida where they had moved following a successful career owning diners in Manhattan, New York. Upon entering the lobby I saw the photo board featuring the seven centenarians who also lived there. That was a clear message to me that our demographics are changing. You might not live until 100, but it is likely that you'll have many years of living in retirement to finance.

Living to 100 may actually become the norm. According to the Census Bureau, by 2050 the number of centenarians around the world is expected to grow to 1,000,000. When I recently mentioned this statistic to a client, he stated with a grin: "A majority of the cars on the road will always have their blinker on and everyone will eat dinner at 4 p.m."

My dear Great Aunt Lila showing me her friends over the age of 100.

Longevity means that planning for retirement will take on more importance than ever before. If we live to 100 rather than

80, the remaining six risks could have a damaging impact on our retirement nest egg. Of course, the key to a well-financed retirement circles right back to the financial planning process discussed later in the book. Since today's advancements in medicine, technology and personal health are allowing retirees to live longer, a solid retirement plan should provide a lifetime income stream that accounts not only for traditional life expectancy, but well beyond. Lifetime income components are necessary in order to ensure that retirees' assets stand the test of time. Given these facts, a critical component of your retirement planning focus needs to address the probability of success. It is imperative to know whether your income is going to outlive you or whether you are likely to outlive your income.

"If we take a late retirement and an early death, we'll just squeak by."

Your health has a lot to do with whether your money will last as long as you do. Of course, we can only control that to a certain extent. So in addition to taking care of our bodies, we need to ensure that we'll have the resources in place should we need more care down the line than we expect.

ADDRESSING RETIREMENT RISK #3: HEALTH/LONG-TERM CARE

Sadly, the escalating costs associated with long-term care during retirement can make the possibility of outliving one's retirement income an unfortunate reality for many. Every one of us hopes to live to a ripe old age, enjoying good health, family and friends along the way. The luckiest of us will. But those who are less fortunate may have to deal with serious and often ongoing health challenges that tend to accompany longevity.

Statistics reveal that as we age, there is an increased probability of our eventually needing assistance with the most basic activities of daily living, such as bathing, dressing, and eating. This type of care—regardless of whether it's in-home or at a facility—does not come cheap. This is a topic that has certainly been making national headlines. Though everyone hopes for the best, your health during retirement is unpredictable.

The truth is that most of us will need long-term care in our golden years. As unsettling as it is to consider the possibility of needing daily assistance, planning for those potential needs now can save a lot of money and heartache later. For a couple turning 65, there is a 75 percent chance that one of them will need long-term care and yet fewer than half have taken steps to prepare for this possibility. How will they pay for long-term care? Most Americans are grossly underfunded for their retirement and do not have enough in general savings. The average cost of a nursing home ranges from $85,000 to $120,000 a year, while hiring an aide to spend an average of six hours a day in the home can start around $40,000 a year.

At age 65, you qualify for the country's largest health insurance plan: Medicare. But there's a catch. Many wrongly believe that savings and government programs such as Medicare and Medicaid will cover the tab if needed. The biggest shock for people entering the Medicare system is learning that it won't pay for custodial care in a nursing home. Medicare was designed to pay for acute illnesses and medical treatments. If you slip on the ice during your years of retirement and need a hip replacement, Medicare will take care of this procedure, but it won't pay for someone to feed you or help you dress. So if you start suffering from dementia and you forget to turn off the stove and almost burn down your house, or if you can no longer bathe yourself anymore, you are not covered. Unless you have someone to care for you, you will wind up in an assisted-living facility to the tune of $70,000 a year, which you'll have to pay for yourself. Only when you have spent all but your last few thousand will you qualify for Medicaid, which will then pay the nursing home bills. Even then, the rules are very complex. For example, you can give away money to your spouse or children to become poor enough to go on Medicaid, but you have to get rid of it five years before you enter a nursing home. This explains why family members provide most long-term care, and why there are 52 million Americans who function as unpaid caregivers.

If you are among the lucky minority, your former employer may offer continued health coverage for its retirees. However if you're like the majority of Americans, this type of coverage will be unavailable. Therefore, if you plan to retire before you become eligible for Medicare, you will be responsible for purchasing personal coverage to fill the gap.

Even if you are eligible for Medicare, you need to allow for out-of-pocket costs to pay for premiums as well as services outside the plan's scope, such as vision, hearing, dental, and podiatric care. Considering that most seniors need these types of care, the costs can add up. According to a non-partisan report published in December 2006, the average senior can expect to pay 27 percent of his or her income toward health care. Therefore, it is of great importance to figure in anticipated medical expenditures when working through your retirement budget.

Clearly many people underestimate the need and cost of long-term care. Why? I find that many people are in denial or believe their children will look after them. Yet in many cases, family members may not live near them or have the means to support them. Even if they do, most of us would rather not be a burden to our loved ones.

Since Medicare does not cover long-term care and many people can't afford to pay for long-term care out of pocket without depleting their retirement nest egg, many pre-retirees are opting to buy long-term care insurance policies. Depending on the contract and issuing company, these policies usually begin paying the costs associated with long-term care once you become unable to independently perform several of the activities of daily living.

This coverage can free you from worries about extended medical care or potentially having to rely on your family members for care or money. Long-term care insurance will provide you and your family with peace of mind before and after needing long-term care. It also works to:

- Protect your assets and preserve an estate for your heirs.
- Enable you to provide yourself or your spouse with the best quality medical care.
- Help you preserve your financial and individual independence. It is important to keep in mind that coverage is about preserving independence—not losing it.

Unfortunately, many do not think about this insurance until they need it.

Although most people recognize the value of long-term care insurance, often the expense of buying a stand-alone policy deters them from seeking coverage. Some insurers now offer an alternative in the form of a long-term care or living care rider that can be attached to a permanent life insurance policy. If the owner ever requires care, the rider makes it possible to accelerate the death benefit of the insurance contract to pay for qualified costs. I suggest becoming educated on the ins and outs of long-term care so you can make an informed decision on what is most appropriate for you.

But Wait, There's More

This is just the start when it comes to putting together your Retirement Income Survival Kit™. As we'll see in the next chapter, to succeed you have to fully understand what you're up against and then act accordingly.

Chapter 6

ROUNDING OUT YOUR RETIREMENT
INCOME SURVIVAL KIT™

Hit the ball over the fence
and you can take your time going around the bases.

—*John W. Roper*

When you know where you're starting from and where you going, and you mitigate the risks along the way, you can take advantage of opportunities. I would discover in New Zealand just how profoundly that adage can impact one's life.

I landed in Auckland after an overnight flight. The sun was just rising. I was excited to be in the "land of the long white cloud" as the native Maoris refer to their homeland. New Zealand is the friendliest developed country I have ever visited. Where else in the world do they hand you a cup of coffee or tea as they sincerely welcome you through customs? Just as I exited baggage claim, half-awake, a frazzled young German man approached me.

"Do you want to buy my car?" he asked in a frantic tone. "I make you a very good price!"

His anxiety was obvious. He was scheduled to board a flight back to Frankfurt that morning and had not yet sold his 1956 Morris Minor Van.

I listened to my gut and thought, *Sure, I will take a look at your car. What do I have to lose?*

The vintage car had some rust and looked a bit worn, but it was oozing with character. With the steering wheel on the English (right) side and paddy wagon doors in the back, it just brought a smile to my face. Similar to investing, this was a matter of making a calculated decision at the right time. I thought to myself, *If the car takes me just up to the Bay of Islands located 150 miles to the north and back again, that alone would be worth a couple hundred dollars.* I offered the man $200. He gladly took the money and handed me the keys with no exchange of paperwork, title or anything else.

Sitting on top of my Morrie on the west coast of New Zealand, 1991.

As I drove my latest purchase in a place I had always dreamed of traveling, I felt as free as an uncaged parrot. Not only did the car's 948cc, 37-horsepower engine get me up to 90 Mile Beach and back, over the next several weeks it transported me and some newfound friends all over the North Island. It did not take me long to learn, however, that the only time an old English car does not leak oil is when there is no oil in the engine. Of course the Morris Minor, affectionately identified by Kiwis as a Morrie, had a lot of other quirks and idiosyncrasies. But she had character and style, and I was proud and excited to call her mine.

It was now time to visit the South Island, known for its snow-capped mountains, towering fiords, verdant rain forests, rugged beaches and pristine glacial lakes. Even though I knew that the Morrie's engine could surrender the white flag at any time, the joy she had already provided me coupled with thoughts of adventures to come tipped the balance in her favor. I spent an additional $200 (the same amount I had paid for the car) to transport her on a ferry through the Marlborough Sounds to the South Island. Over the next two months, I crisscrossed this island/theme park, participating in every fun antic I could find. This included leaping off the world's first commercial bungee jumping bridge, tandem parapenting off the sheer Bob's Peak in Queenstown, white-water rafting, jet-boat riding through the canyons of the Shotover River, tubing the river in Waitomo Caves, swimming with dolphins, skiing down an active volcano, and hiking some of the world's most spectacular "tramps," including the Milford Track which author James Michener referred to as the most beautiful place on earth.

The car enhanced the experiences. To this day I am still friends with people I met through Morrie when I picked them up hitchhiking. When it was time to leave this beautiful country, I sold Morrie for $600 to three recent arrivals from Savannah, Georgia, who were ready to start their own journey Down Under. I was quite sad to say farewell to my friend who had opened up so many opportunities for me. I felt just as sad to leave New Zealand, where I felt so comfortable and at home.

Little did I know that just a few years later I would meet a New Zealand woman who would become my wife and the mother of our two children. When I met Jill in Telluride, Colorado, my New Zealand escapade and the fact that I had owned a Morris Minor caught her attention. During her youth, her parents had each owned a Morrie. How could she not fall in love?

A Life of Saturdays

Soon after marrying, I sold my driveway sealing business. Jill and I moved to Bend, Oregon, a town that reminded us of New Zealand because of its beautiful scenery and friendly people. Never before had we been to a locale where almost all the residents had come from somewhere else, having made a conscious decision to live, raise their children or retire there. Over the years friends and family members would approach me for financial advice, as they knew investing had become a passion for me and that I had continued to educate myself on the subject. I had an inner sense and a hunch that my next calling was to become a financial advisor, so I jumped in and got my license. I did not know a soul in our idyllic hometown but I knew I could be of benefit to others and grow a successful practice over time. Within months, I had set up a financial planning office in downtown Bend.

One morning I looked out my new office window and I could not believe my eyes. A Morris Minor! The distinctive front grille was unmistakable. I immediately ran outside to appreciate it firsthand. It was a convertible! I had no idea they made a topless model. Furthermore, I had never seen this British icon in the States. It was in beautiful condition. It even had the steering wheel on the English side! It was love at first sight. I looked all around for the owner of the car to no avail. I had an appointment, which was not an everyday occurrence at that time, so I left a note on the windshield that read: *I used to own this same car in New Zealand. If you ever want to sell it, please call me.* Sadly, by the time my appointment was over, the Morrie was gone.

A year later I was mowing my lawn when my wife told me that someone was on the phone for me. At the other end I heard, "David, this is your lucky day. I am selling my Morris Minor." It took me a moment to put the pieces together and remember the car I had spotted downtown some twelve months prior. That same day we were in his garage across town with our recently born daughter Sophie. My heart was pumping. Just looking at the car brought back so many wonderful memories from my New Zealand exploits. I knew Jill was recalling her childhood in New Zealand. The owner, John, shared his story. Years earlier he had shipped the car from England to Bend for his Japanese girlfriend, who had named the car Peaches. Now he was retiring as a doctor from St. Charles Hospital in order to sail his boat from Portland to, of all places, New Zealand.

I proceeded to share with him a photo of the Morrie I had previously owned in New Zealand, along with the fact that Jill had taught English in Japan for two years. This was more than a coincidence we thought. John suggested we take Peaches for a spin and even placed Sophie's car seat in the back. The moment I got behind the right-side steering wheel I felt at home. We drove the car right into our garage, as I knew it was going to be ours. We got out of the car, acknowledged that she had found her new home, and then drove back to make it official.

When we returned to John's home, he could see the grins on our faces. He proceeded to show us every receipt, from shipping and restoration to replacement parts and labor. He had probably invested more money into the Morrie than she was worth. He expressed how delighted he was to see our adoration for Peaches and how he had been waiting to pass this car on to the right people who would appreciate her. We were those people. Then he pulled out the receipts from the prior year, which did not add up to more than a few thousand dollars. If we simply paid that amount, the car would be ours. In disbelief, I immediately wrote him a check and drove our new family member into her warm new home. She looked so good in our garage.

Peaches, which I drive to work most summer days, has brought a continual stream of serendipity and good fortune into our lives. For the better part of a decade she was the face of my financial practice as her non-ostentatious, adventurous spirit shared a message about the road to financial independence. It was as though she said:

- *Envision your life's journey.*
- *See yourself in the driver's seat.*
- *Make the right turns on your financial journey.*

Peaches is a dear friend. I can come home from a long day at work and take her for a spin and all of my concerns evaporate. When we take her on a family ride and park downtown, she attracts a crowd of smiling, curious faces. Peaches is not just another pretty classic car, she is the symbol for me of a plethora of life lessons.

Peaches, the former face of my financial practice.

Henry David Thoreau wrote:

If one advances confidently in the direction of his dreams, and endeavors to live the life which he has imagined, he will meet with a success unexpected in common hours.

What this means to me is that if you focus on what it is you want in life and if you continually do good, when you least expect it the worthy things in life that motivate you will suddenly appear.

Peaches also offers me some other life lessons:
- Like Peaches, one does not need to be flamboyant or showy to get positive attention.
- If you treat others well, they will treat you well. Peaches recently celebrated her 57th birthday and is still a beauty because she is well maintained and loved.
- There are no accidents in our lives. Everything happens for a purpose. What are the chances of a German tourist passing a car on to me that would come back to me decades later in my new hometown of Bend, after I'd met and married a woman from New Zealand who also has a history with such automobiles?

The biggest lesson Peaches has imparted to me, however, has to do with finances. Here it is:

If you look after your money the way you would an old beloved car, you can live the life you have always imagined.

Peaches, Bend, Oregon, 2013.

My New Zealand experiences proved to me that what we think about expands. As you plan your years of financial independence, you must make sure that your financial planning expands with your vision. That means rounding out your retirement income survival kit because, as you already know, failure is not an option. That starts with evaluating and safeguarding yourself against market risk.

Addressing Retirement RISK #4: MARKET RISK

We don't like to think about markets heading south, but economic recessions have occurred all throughout the history of modern economics and always will. We average one almost every nine years. We have experienced 10 recessions between 1945 and 2013. The average duration of these recessions is 10 months. Many people have referred to our last economic setback as the "Great Recession," since by many measures it was the most severe post-World War II recession we've had. It remains to be seen whether this name will stick, as it has been applied to numerous prior recessions. I hope we don't ever experience another recession like this last one. But as you plan your exciting years of financial independence, you need to have an investment game plan in place that will enable you to withstand future recessions, because they will come. If you were to retire at age 65 and live to age 90, statistically you would experience three recessions during your retirement years.

With the ups and downs of market returns being a concern for every investor these days, it is important to assess retirement risks early and to regularly protect against an adverse downturn. Without sufficient risk management, one year of adverse returns can cause a great deal of insecurity in the long-term success of even the best-planned retirement portfolio.

Now let me ask you a question.

If the market loses 50 percent one year and then increases 50 percent the following year, where are you?

I love asking that question because without fail most people will say that you are back where you started. In actual fact, your portfolio has experienced a 25 percent decline.

Let's test the math. After $1 million loses 50 percent of its value you are left with $500,000. When $500,000 increases by 50 percent you have $750,000, which means that 25 percent of the portfolio has disappeared. Can you imagine what would have happened had you retired in 2001 and experienced this scenario twice? 2002 and 2008 constituted two of the three worst performing years in S&P history. As we work our way out of our current economic woes, many have already forgotten the results of the dot-com crisis and 9/11. That's a mistake since market risk will always be an element of investing.

To see just how much of an adverse impact a down market can have, consider the following:

CASE STUDY:
A 65-year-old couple needs to withdraw an annual income of $40,000 from their $1 million nest egg. If in the first year of retirement the market falls 10, 20, or 30 percent, the portfolio has a great deal of stress to overcome in order to produce the needed income and also maintain principal.

Let's assume that in the first year of retirement, the clients' portfolio returned negative 10 percent while they were taking distributions. The portfolio would need to earn a net average return of 8.13 percent for the next five years to return to the $1,000,000 principal balance in the account. But what if instead of having a negative 10 percent return in year one, we have a negative 30 percent return? How does that affect the portfolio and the need for growth in subsequent years of retirement? In order to overcome that loss and get back to where it began, the portfolio will need to gain a net average return 14.69 percent for the next five years for the account value to reach the initial $1,000,000.

During the accumulation phase when investors are saving for retirement, their focus is often on returns. In the process they are benchmarking an arbitrary index. Once we hit the Fragile Risk Zone and enter the distribution phase, I believe it is essential to shift our focus from returns to lack of risk and volatility. We should no longer benchmark an index but benchmark our beach house or desired lifestyle. The numbers speak for themselves. If your portfolio were to drop 50 percent, you would need a 100 percent return to break even and recoup your losses. If your portfolio lost 20 percent, you would need a 25 percent return to break even. That's not a risk you can afford to run, even if you think you can outsmart the market.

Many investors like to time the markets. I was recently introduced to a new client who shared his perceived success story of such market timing. In an excited tone he explained how he liquidated his entire equity portfolio in October of 2007 when the Dow Jones Industrial Average, a price-weighted average of 30 large companies on the New York Stock Exchange, was near its peak-closing price at that time of 14,164. He went on to give details about how the Dow hit a market low of 6,443.27 on March 6, 2009, having lost over 54 percent of its value since the October 2007 high.

I asked him when he got back in the market. He stated in a less fervent tone that he had not done that yet as he was waiting for the markets to decline first. I informed him that the markets had since experienced momentous growth and the Dow has well more than doubled over this period of time achieving a new all-time high. I didn't have to add that he had lost out. By the time I was done, he knew.

When you time the markets you have to be lucky twice. You must not only get out of the markets at the right time but you need to get back in at the right time. This gentleman was lucky once but not twice, and consequently now faces a serious dilemma. To be successful over the long term, it is time in the markets not timing the markets that counts.

For better or worse, investors may have control when it comes to timing the markets but they have little to no control of the market unpredictability that creates the market's fondness for volatility. If we could accurately predict the size and timing of the market's movements, there would be no uncertainty and no volatility. However, the higher returns that have accompanied this enduring environment of volatility would probably vanish. Because some people are willing to accept a higher level of principal risk along with uncertainty, they have invested in equity-based funds and have historically been rewarded with higher returns over the long term than those who have been invested in safer and less volatile, fixed-income investments. As returns increase, however, so too do the volatility and risk. This is the paradox by which market volatility has been defined.

An investment's performance usually has a direct correlation to that investment's volatility. As the return potential of a specific investment grows, the likelihood that the investment could experience a loss of principal correspondingly increases. So it is crucial to focus more on lack of risk and volatility than returns as you approach the Fragile Risk Zone.

Ironically, as the economy continues to grow and a foundation of positive momentum takes place, we are faced with a series of challenges here at home, including fiscal cutbacks by federal, state and local governments, Social Insecurity, steep oil prices, a polarized Congress and, sadly, terrorism. Global concerns also have an impact on us including the European debt crisis, nuclear fears in North Korea and Iran, and continued unrest in places like Syria. This creates significant fear and corresponding market volatility.

What factors have the greatest influence on an investment's volatility? Generally, an investment's classification is determined by its level of volatility. Fixed income or cash-based investment funds are said to be the least volatile, while small cap and international stock funds are said to be among the most volatile. Between these two classes are bonds, large and mid-cap stock funds, and funds that combine characteristics from each of these classes. Because the rate of return on fixed income-based funds tends to be lower, however, they are generally more susceptible to inflation rate risk, which was discussed earlier.

Those are just the start of the factors that need to be considered when making your financial plan. One of the most important and least understood risks you face in retirement is the Sequence of Returns.

ADDRESSING RETIREMENT RISK #5: THE SEQUENCE OF RETURNS

As if market risk isn't enough of a challenge in retirement planning, when you experience gains or losses—or the order in which you receive your returns—can have a significant impact on your retirement portfolio. Either one can mean the difference between having enough income in retirement and running out of money too soon.

The transition from the retirement accumulation phase during the working years to the retirement distribution phase creates a clarifying and critical change. In the accumulation phase, the focus is usually on the average of investment returns. As individuals move to the retirement distribution phase, the sequence of the investment returns becomes the focus and is critical to the overall success of the financial plan. Setbacks in the sequence of returns could potentially be the biggest hazard you will face in retirement.

Consider the two charts on the following page. I consider the investor represented by the left chart to be the lucky investor and the investor to the right the unlucky investor. They share a great many similarities. They are 65 years of age and have account balances of $800,000. Their accounts are experiencing an 8 percent average rate of return. They are each taking a 6 percent annual withdrawal (6 percent of $800,000 = $48,000). One would think that they would have the same chance for a successful retirement, and yet the lucky investor is able to grow his account value significantly over time while taking his 6 percent withdrawals each year while the unlucky investor is broke just part way through retirement.

How can this be? What is the difference?

CHART 1 - LUCKY INVESTOR				CHART 2 - UNLUCKY INVESTOR			
"UP" MARKET				"DOWN" MARKET			
Age	Annual Return	Annual Withdrawal	Year-End Value	Age	Annual Return	Annual Withdrawal	Year-End Value
65			$ 800,000	65			$ 800,000
66	5%	$ 48,000	$ 792,000	66	-22%	$ 48,000	$ 567000
67	28%	$ 48,000	$ 965,760	67	-12%	$ 48,000	$ 458,880
68	22%	$ 48,000	$ 1,130,227	68	-9%	$ 48,000	$ 369,581
69	-5%	$ 48,000	$ 1,025,715	69	17%	$ 48,000	$ 384,409
70	38%	$ 48,000	$ 1,367,487	70	22%	$ 48,000	$ 420,979
71	19%	$ 48,000	$ 1,579,310	71	6%	$ 48,000	$ 398,238
72	23%	$ 48,000	$ 1,894,551	72	-15%	$ 48,000	$ 290,503
73	9%	$ 48,000	$ 2,017,061	73	9%	$ 48,000	$ 268,648
74	31%	$ 48,000	$ 2,594,350	74	14%	$ 48,000	$ 258,258
75	23%	$ 48,000	$ 3,143,050	75	25%	$ 48,000	$ 274,823
76	34%	$ 48,000	$ 4,163,687	76	14%	$ 48,000	$ 265,298
77	-26%	$ 48,000	$ 3,033,129	77	5%	$ 48,000	$ 230,563
78	-15%	$ 48,000	$ 2,530,159	78	-15%	$ 48,000	$ 147,979
79	5%	$ 48,000	$ 2,608,667	79	-26%	$ 48,000	$ 61,504
80	14%	$ 48,000	$ 2,925,881	80	34%	$ 48,000	$ 34,416
81	25%	$ 48,000	$ 3,609,351	81	23%	$ 42,332	$ 0
82	14%	$ 48,000	$ 4,066,660	82	31%		
83	9%	$ 48,000	$ 4,384,659	83	9%		
84	-15%	$ 48,000	$ 3,678,961	84	23%		
85	6%	$ 48,000	$ 3,851,698	85	19%		
86	22%	$ 48,000	$ 4,651,072	86	38%		
87	17%	$ 48,000	$ 5,393,754	87	-5%		
88	-9%	$ 48,000	$ 4,860,316	88	22%		
89	-12%	$ 48,000	$ 4,229,078	89	28%		
90	-22%	$ 48,000	$ 3,250,681	90	5%		
	8%		$ 3,250,681		8%		

The only difference between Chart 1 and Chart 2 is the sequence of the returns. The returns share the exact same numbers; I just reversed their order. Whereas the lucky investor began his retirement with positive rates of return—5 percent, 28 percent and 22 percent—the unlucky investor experienced these same returns at the end of his life. Whereas the unlucky investor begain his retirement with three negative years of returns—-22 percent, -12 percent and -9 percent—the lucky investor experienced these same returns at the end of his life. I find most investors are unaware that experiencing negative returns early in retirement distribution can have a potentially devastating impact on account balances. The fact is that in retirement, the difference between success and failure often comes down to the timing of returns.

What should you take away about this relatively unknown and potentially lethal financial risk?

- When planning for your years of financial independence, understand that using historical averages is misleading when looked at alone. Be careful when an analysis states that you should achieve your goals by obtaining a specific rate of return. In most cases this statement has not taken into account the sequence of returns.

- It can be dangerous to have a retirement projection using a straight-line rate of return without factoring in bad timing. Even though a portfolio may return above-average numbers, consideration must be given to when those returns take place. Monte Carlo simulations can greatly benefit retirement planning.

Monte Carlo and Financial Planning

The name Monte Carlo naturally brings to mind the gambling mecca located in Monaco. The use of the name in this case is no coincidence. When it comes to estimating one's retirement, this statistical-based analysis tool is a true advancement over past options. It takes into account real-world experiences in a way that other planning methods don't. So it can be used to better your odds of retiring with the funds you want and need.

At its most basic, a Monte Carlo simulation allows us to determine the likelihood of different outcomes by running thousands of scenarios using specific parameters. It is very powerful for clients to know their probability of achieving all their financial goals or of potentially outliving their money. Given the unpredictable nature of the stock market, these simulations help us model how a particular portfolio will perform under various market conditions. This helps clients make more informed investment decisions when determining appropriate portfolio allocations, market returns, spending patterns and withdrawal rates (the focus of the next section) in order to help ensure that their nest eggs last a lifetime.

For example, if your retirement plan that does not incorporate Monte Carlo simulations estimates a 7 percent return for your retirement portfolio, that plan can only illustrate a straight-line return, meaning an exact 7 percent return each and every year. We know this is not reality. Even though your portfolio may average that 7 percent return over time, Monte Carlo can help us determine the likelihood of success knowing that the portfolio will experience good and not-so-good years.

Since you know about the sequence of returns, you can see how powerful this tool can be for your future. That's why it is very important to incorporate Monte Carlo into your retirement planning—and you don't even need a passport to do so!

Now let's look at how your funds are allocated.

ADDRESSING RETIREMENT RISK #6: WITHDRAWAL SUSTAINABILITY

When it comes to retirement planning, a common question clients ask is, "What dollar amount should I have saved in order to retire safely?" The answer should be based on multiple factors such as the allocation of your retirement account, inflation, and amount of income needed. A comprehensive income-distribution plan emphasizes the appropriate asset allocation and enables you to build a retirement income plan that increases the chances of your savings lasting throughout retirement. I call this the Probability of Sustainability.

As discussed earlier with my "Gilligan's Island" analogy, in today's world a million dollars will not enable one to live in a mansion, own a yacht or send three children to Ivy League universities. Investing $1 million to cover even basic living expenses is not an easy task. This may seem difficult to fathom, but let's take a close look at the 4 percent rule for retirement withdrawal. While this rule is not an exact science, it can provide investors with a 30,000-foot view. Morningstar's comprehensive research states that if you have a balanced portfolio in retirement made up of stocks and bonds, you have a 97 percent probability of not outliving your resources over a twenty-five-year retirement, as long as you live on only 4 percent of the principle.

In short, you need stocks in your portfolio if you want to live well, but bonds if you want to sleep well. Panic sets in for many when they see the statistics drop to just better than a 50 percent chance of success with a 6 percent withdrawal. The recommended 4 percent withdrawal from $1 million equates to a $40,000 annual income stream, and this has not factored in either Uncle Sam's portion or inflation.

Even worse, in today's new world economy of extremely low and artificial interest rates, banks are offering negligible returns on deposits. A 1 or 2 percent return would yield $10,000 or $20,000 annually on that $1 million. This would place even a single person in the poverty zone.

Let's see how this works in real life.

EXAMPLE:

Steve, 55, estimates that he will live no longer than age 95. He is currently contemplating retiring at age 60 or 65. Steve is trying to determine how sustainable $100,000 of income will be if he retired with an anticipated $2,000,000 at age 60 or $2,500,000 at age 65. Steve's current allocation in his portfolio is a 40/60 blend between equities and bonds; he does not anticipate changing his allocation in the future. For this example, I assumed that inflation in the future would remain around 3 percent.

Based on the information above, we can anticipate that if Steve retires in five years at age 60 with $2,000,000 in savings, he will have a 32 percent probability of success in retirement. This figure is calculated by taking the income divided by the nest egg ($100,000/$2,000,000), which is 5 percent, and then cross-referencing that figure with the 35-year sustainability chart below for the applicable portfolio allocation (40/60).

35 - Year Retirement Stock / Bond Mix					
	100/0	80/20	60/40	40/60	20/80
3%	86%	89%	91%	93%	93%
4%	70%	71%	70%	65%	52%
5%	53%	51%	44%	32%	13%
6%	38%	33%	23%	11%	1%
7%	26%	19%	11%	3%	0%
8%	16%	11%	4%	0%	0%

If Steve decided to wait 10 years and retire at age 65 with a $2,500,000 nest egg, he would have an 80 percent probability of success in retirement. This figure is calculated by taking the income divided by the nest egg ($100,000/$2,500,000) which is 4 percent, and then cross-referencing that figure with the 30-year sustainability chart below for the applicable portfolio allocation (40/60).

	30 - Year Retirement Stock / Bond Mix					
		100/0	80/20	60/40	40/60	20/80
	3%	90%	93%	96%	98%	99%
	4%	77%	79%	80%	80%	74%
Initial Withdrawal Amount	5%	60%	59%	55%	46%	28%
	6%	44%	40%	32%	19%	5%
	7%	31%	25%	16%	6%	0%
	8%	20%	14%	7%	1%	0%

For Steve it was essential to know and understand this information well in advance of his retirement so that he could make an informed decision. By delaying his retirement for five years, his probability of success increased dramatically, offering him and his wife considerable peace of mind. But he still has to account for an annual tax hit.

ADDRESSING RETIREMENT RISK #7: TAXATION

It has been said that the only two certainties in life are death and taxes. So it's important to consider how taxes affect retirement savings. With expectations of rising rates over time, tax deferral should become increasingly more important.

Tax deferral has two major benefits: Savings grow unhindered by taxes, enhancing the compounding effect. If savings are accumulated during peak working years and you are able to delay paying taxes until you retire, you may come out ahead as you will potentially be in a lower tax bracket once you start pulling out that money. Of course, that assumes that you don't lose tax deductions along the way.

The increased compounding of savings inside of a tax-deferred vehicle can be substantial. Assume two investors each have an account balance of $1 million with an investment horizon of 35 years until retirement. John invested 50 percent into the S&P 500 and 50 percent into a mix of investment-grade bonds in a taxable investment account. Kathy invested into the exact same allocations; however, she did so in a tax-deferred account. Because tax deferral enables your money to work much harder for you, at retirement, Kathy has seen her account value grow $6.6 million greater than John's account value based on current tax rates.

Upon entering the income distribution phase of your life, there are a number of taxation factors such as Social Security and Required Minimum Distributions (RMD) to take into consideration. The rules for Social Security benefits are especially convoluted and confusing. Taxes are triggered for Social Security recipients when their Modified Adjusted Gross Income (MAGI) exceeds specified amounts. To calculate whether MAGI surpasses the tax-triggering thresholds, retirees must consider income from various sources such as: pensions, dividends, capital gains, rents, RMDs from traditional IRAs, 401(k)s as well as tax-exempt interest from municipal bonds.

A basic way to calculate this is take your Social Security Benefit ÷ 2 + ordinary income + dividends + interest from municipal bonds = MAGI. If this number is below $32,000 then Social Security benefits are not taxed. If MAGI is between $32,000 and $44,000, up to 50 percent of Social Security benefits are taxed. And if MAGI surpasses $44,000 for joint filers, up to 85 percent of benefits are taxed. The goal is to minimize your future tax liability. The primary challenge is that all of your qualified retirement accounts will be taxed as ordinary income and be included in your MAGI.

That's why it is a good time to have lots of money inside Roth IRAs and why more and more retirees have been converting their Traditional IRAs into Roth IRAs. Although this means a tax consequence for them now, it could benefit them significantly over time. Here is why:

- Roth IRAs do not have RMDs requiring you to take distributions and pay taxes from age 70 ½ onward.

- Now is a prudent time to convert to a Roth IRA as taxes are only expected to increase in the future. Consider paying the taxes now at the lower rates.
- By having your funds in Roth IRAs, your legacy to your heirs will be tax efficient.
- A Roth IRA enables your investments to grow tax free. This growth as well as the entire distribution will be free of all taxes and not be factored into your MAGI. The intent is to lower your Traditional IRA value where you may not have to pay tax on 85 percent of your Social Security benefit as well as ordinary income tax on every distribution taken from your Traditional IRA.

You'll also want to talk about Required Minimum Distributions with your tax advisor. Like all tax laws, those surrounding RMDs can be confusing. The IRS has enabled your qualified retirement accounts to grow at accelerated rates by deferring the taxes on your investments. However, by the time you reach the age of 70 ½, the IRS seems to feel that it is about time they start to receive some additional income. How do they accomplish this? They require you to withdraw at least a portion of the funds in your qualified retirement accounts over the remainder of your lifetime; every dollar withdrawn from an IRA is taxed at ordinary income tax rates. These RMDs are determined by dividing your prior year-end market value of your retirement assets by your life expectancy.

If the distributions do not occur in accordance with federal guidelines, heavy penalties are imposed, making your understanding of these distribution rules increasingly important. If you fail to comply with these rules, the IRS will impose a

50 percent penalty in addition to withholding the taxes that would have been due from the distribution. So taking the time to understand these rules is essential for building your own Retirement Income Survival Kit™.

Your retirement distribution plan, however, needs to cover more than the money that's going out, whether to you or to the Tax Man. It also needs to factor in the legacy you would like to leave behind for the people and organizations you care about most.

ADDRESSING RETIREMENT RISK #8: LEGACY

A portion of my clients express to me that they have done a great deal financially for their children over the years from paying for all or a portion of their college education and weddings to covering the down payment on their first homes. With their grown offspring successful in their own careers and financially self-sufficient, it is now Mom and Dad's opportunity to focus on fun and adventure. For them retirement is a time to travel the world, purchase their wants and desires, and of course enjoy the grandchildren. If they die with a dollar to their name, they feel like they have won.

For another portion of my clientele, leaving behind a financial legacy is a primary objective, even if that means reducing their standard of living in retirement. If your objectives are similar, it is important to include the legacy you would like to leave behind in your financial goals and to balance your funding of retirement income with provisions for your intentions.

PUTTING IT ALL TOGETHER

Creating your retirement distribution plan involves analyzing your exposure to the eight key retirement risks that you, and indeed all retirees, face. It is then important to make a decision as to how you wish to address each of them. Generally these decisions fall into four categories:

AVOID
Eliminate / Withdraw

RETAIN
Accept / Budget

REDUCE
Optimize / Mitigate

TRANSFER
Share / Insure

As retirees enter the distribution phase of their lives, the emphasis often shifts from tax deferral to the transfer of their estate to their heirs in the most tax-efficient manner possible. Without proper planning Uncle Sam can easily become your primary beneficiary. I will share a few specific strategies to help you avoid this in Chapter 10.

In the meantime, with the proper study of retirement, a concept I refer to as *Retirementology*, your legacy wishes can come to fruition upon your passing and serendipity can be prevalent during your years of financial independence.

Chapter 7

RETIREMENTOLOGY

It is not the years in your life but the life in your years.

—*Abraham Lincoln*

S trategic preparation that enables you to live your life as fully as you want is an essential element in the science of retirement because, that's right, failure is just not an option. With the right planning, you even make room for a little luck to impact your life.

I met renowned ski filmmaker Warren Miller in 1982, back in the days when he still presented his witty and humorous narrative in person. His annual film that year, *SnoWonder,* showcased the extraordinary talents of world-class adventure skiers including Glen Plake. Miller used a helicopter like a taxi, dropping him atop incredibly steep peaks in the Rockies of British Columbia. From there they accessed some of the world's lightest virgin powder over varying terrain that ranged from glaciers and alpine bowls to steep chutes and glades studded with trees. I watched the big screen in disbelief. That vicarious experience instantly topped my bucket list of must-dos during my life.

Helicopter skiing, British Columbia, 2012.

But helicopter skiing is extravagantly expensive, so it wasn't going to happen anytime soon. Fast forward to 2012. Just a few months before losing my kind and gentle father-in-law Hugh to pancreatic cancer, I lost a very dear friend Jan to the same horrific illness. The day after Jan's heroic battle ended, an overwhelming feeling of sorrow weighed down upon me. Just then a close friend and ski companion, Bob Engelbrecht, invited me to join him helicopter skiing in the Selkirk and Monashee Mountain Ranges of the Canadian Rockies. Bob is a former helicopter pilot from Alaska and coincidentally was planning this excursion with Canadian Mountain Holiday (CMH), the same company used by Warren Miller Films and credited with starting heli-skiing in 1965 in British Columbia.

As you can imagine, there is nothing financially sensible about such an escapade. Considering the timing, however, I felt this was fate reminding me to celebrate life because it's way too short. I knew I had to go.

Bob and I landed in Calgary to meet up with our group the evening before a seven-hour bus ride north to the Gothics Lodge. Our timing could not have been any better as the snow gods were blessing us with bottomless powder, so much so that just three hours up the Trans-Canada Highway in the town of Golden the roads were impassable. CMH decided to fly us in from there, which provided Bob and me with a glorious 45-minute helicopter ride over some of the most isolated and breathtaking scenery imaginable. It also saved us four additional hours in the bus.

That evening I looked at the names on the guest list with interest to see what parts of the world the expedition's other participants would be joining us from. As expected, I found an international list of names from England, Iceland, Australia, New Zealand, Canada and the United States. With great surprise and fortuitous good fortune, I also read the names Charles Schwab, Jr. and Charles Schwab III on the list.

Could it be?

Of course, it had to be!

It was.

Bob and I would spend the next week in the same helicopter with the Schwabs, whose investment brokerage firm is one of the world's largest and most respected. Right off the bat Sandy, as Charles Jr. is referred to, and his son Charlie were a pleasure to get to know. We shared unforgettable experiences of skiing down mountain peaks only accessible by helicopter by day and then investment discussions and life stories over delicious red wine in the evening. Serendipity was taking charge and the trip was only getting started.

During our first afternoon, we practiced finding hidden objects in the deep snow using avalanche transceivers, probes and shovels. There is a certain protocol to follow in the unfortunate occurrence of someone becoming buried in an avalanche. Before skiers begin their descent, they activate their transceiver, causing the device to emit a low-power pulsed beacon signal. In such an event, those not caught in the barrage of snow immediately switch their transceivers from transmit to search mode so they can locate their trapped companion using a series of audio signals. Little did Bob and I know at the time that just a couple of days later we would have a true understanding of the importance of such preparation.

I had waited a lifetime for this. I watched the snow piling up outside the window as I prepared my gear in the lodge. Being dropped off by a helicopter on a snow-capped peak many miles away from any sign of civilization was a dream come true. I felt magnanimous as I peered down upon the untouched billowing snow below. I looked at Bob and the Schwabs and said, "It's all yours. Go for it." They didn't argue.

I was right behind them as we pushed off the lip of the bowl, gaining speed and momentum through the trees. The swish of face shots (snow in your face) triggered enormous grins. This was the closest thing to heaven on earth.

Face shots!

Over the ridge just miles away in Revelstoke, CMH has another lodge that was occupied with guests. Their experience that same day had a very different outcome. Imagine the slope just below where your tips hang over the small cornice at the top breaking away. The slope begins to slide with great momentum leaving a laceration in the snow nearly two-feet high. You yell, but the skiers below you don't hear you. The avalanche moves as a single mass, gaining great speed as a cloud of smoke engulfs your companions. You watch in disbelief and bring your hand to your mouth. All you can see are chunks of debris. Then the world is suddenly quiet.

This is what happened the third day of our weeklong ski trip when at 1:35 p.m. we heard "Code Red, Code Red" on the radios strapped to our chests. This kicked off a flurry of emergency radio calls and helicopter trips as our guides made sure we were in a safe place before leaving us on the mountainside and flying away, over the massive ridge, to search for the missing guests. The snow slide had swallowed one skier and partially buried three others who were following their guide down a run dubbed Selkirk. It took only 10 minutes to dig them all out, but it was too late for Greg Sheardown who was pronounced dead on the scene. He was only 45, married with three young boys at home. I was introspective for the remainder of the trip. This unexpected accident brought thoughts of Hugh and Jan to mind. Like Greg Sheardown, they, too, had had so much life ahead of them.

Like so many people, I have lost numerous family members and friends to cancer over the past several years. That has altered the way I look at life and helps ensure that I never take any day for granted. Life is fleeting and it can change in the blink of an eye when you least expect it. We are promised no tomorrows, so it is important to live in the moment. That's exactly why I had signed on for this adventure in British Columbia.

I believe when we stop trying to take life so seriously and make time for fun, serendipity usually takes over. Serendipity is one of my favorite words. It means unexpected good happenings or the fate of finding something good or useful while not specifically searching for it. Meeting the Schwabs is an example of such destiny. These days you have to create your own good fortune. At no time is that truer than in your retirement years.

Retirement today is very different from our parents'. You already know the impact longevity has on your retirement. Now let's discuss how the mindset around retirement has changed over the years and what it means today. According to *Aging and Work in the 21st Century*, in 1950, half the men over 65 remained in the workforce. By 2013 the number was less than 18 percent. It was not that long ago that the average person in our country would retire around the age of 70 and just a few short years later would no longer be with us. In 1900, the average American lived to the not-so-ripe age of 47. Today that number is over 78 and rising.

This trend has led to boredom for many retirees. How much golf can one play? Over time, people begin to miss some of the action and feeling of achievement their working years offered. I see increasing numbers of individuals who are retiring for a period to catch their breath before making the transition to a new chapter in life. Some decide to start that small business they have always dreamed of. I met a couple who opened up a coffee shop because they wanted to be of service to their community; in the process, they made new friends of those customers who visited daily. They launched their new business not because they needed the money, but because this would give them purpose and pleasure. Are they actually retired? Are their lives ending? They certainly don't think so.

The word *retirement* comes from an old French word *retirer*, meaning *to withdraw* or *to take away*. Today when people retire, their focus is not typically on the end. In fact statistics show that many people will spend more than one third of their lives in retirement. So rather than viewing retirement as the withdrawal from work, it may be more accurate to see it as the beginning of a new, even better, life.

Over the years I have replaced the word *retirement* in my practice with the term *financial independence.* What does financial independence mean for you? Have you planned for it? This new generation of aging boomers seems poised to swap that old dream of freedom from work for a new one built around the freedom to work. Home Depot and AARP recently announced a new partnership to recruit older workers for the home renovation giant. They are targeting retirees who couldn't wait to hit the tool shed following a day on the job. The campaign steers them toward trading in retirement for a new vision of what work can be. The slogan: *Passion never retires.*

Graying also means playing for many of today's retirees. Neither young nor old, they are finished with midlife, yet they can look forward to the likelihood of decades of vitality before becoming truly old. What might you rightly aspire to in the next phase? How will you define success in your years of financial independence? Unless you clearly spell that out, you may not get there. Since failure on this front is clearly not an option, let's explore how to make a financial success out of your retirement.

CREATING YOUR HIERARCHY OF NEEDS

If you are like most retirees, you know how much money you have, but you may not have a clear idea of what that money can or can't do for you over the remainder of your life. You have been receiving paychecks from your employers or your business throughout your working years. Now it is essential to create paychecks from your investments. How do you best accomplish this?

If you ever took a Psychology 101 course in school you probably learned about Dr. Abraham Maslow, a renowned American psychologist best known for creating Maslow's Hierarchy of Needs in 1943. His hierarchy is typically displayed in the shape of a mountain. The base of the mountain is made up of the most basic needs, which consist of food, water, sleep, and warmth. Once these lower-level needs have been met, you can move on to the next level of needs, eventually advancing to the more complex needs located toward the summit. As you progress from the base toward the peak, the need for personal esteem and feelings of accomplishment take priority. The zenith is where the need for *self-actualization* occurs. This is when you reach a state of harmony and understanding because you are engaged in achieving your full potential. This level explores your morality and spirituality. For some, spirituality may mean attending a church or synagogue and for others it may mean climbing a mountain. However, it would be very difficult to be self-actualized if your focus was on finding your next meal. This is why Maslow's studies showed that human needs must be fulfilled one level at a time.

So what does this have to do with your financial planning? I have borrowed Dr. Maslow's Hierarchy of Needs to help you create your personalized financial hierarchy and find solutions for the ideal approach to turn your retirement accounts into *paychecks* and *playchecks*. That's exactly what I did for John and Mary, who were recently referred to my practice.

John is a retired surgeon who had been managing a portion of their assets while a national brokerage firm managed the other portion. He shared how almost 50 percent of their wealth was wiped out during the most recent market correction in 2008. Why a retired couple would be invested in such a way that would put so much of their finances at risk is beyond me. Fortunately for them, they had remained affluent despite their market losses. However they were truly terrified after this experience and it showed.

John is a very tall man. He always used to fly first class as it offered him far greater legroom as well as providing Mary and him with the comforts they had grown accustomed to. That had changed with their market losses. Even though they still had prosperity in their lives, their new, strong sense of fear had compelled them to forlornly fly economy when visiting their grandchildren in Europe. This was not only physically uncomfortable for John, it reminded his wife and him of how much money they'd lost. But based on their distress of conceivably outliving their income one day, they had made the decision to spend less no matter how demoralizing.

John and Mary knew how much money they had left, but they did not know what this money could or couldn't do for them over the remaining decades of their lives. They didn't know how much money they should live on each year or where they should take it from. They pondered how their money should be allocated at this stage of their lives, but came up with no answers.

Like most people, including highly educated individuals such as John and Mary, this couple was not familiar with most of the eight key risks individuals face in retirement. We discussed each of these in detail—including inflation, longevity, health, market risks, sequence of returns, withdrawal sustainability, taxation, and legacy—and explored how each risk applied to them. Then John and Mary invested in a RISK Blueprint™ to garner specific answers to all of their questions and create their own personalized hierarchy of needs. Let's follow that part of their financial exploration.

THE BASE OF THE MOUNTAIN: CORE EXPENSES

Maslow shared that one's needs are predetermined in order of importance. The more advanced needs only come into focus once the lower needs are met. As you prepare for your retirement years, the most critical level of your financial mountain is the base, what I refer to as your CORE EXPENSES. These are the required expenditures that all retirees face in their years of financial independence—the costs that cannot be avoided. They include food, clothing, housing, transportation, taxes, insurance and health care. When you consider the detrimental effects of the past recession and the fact that we average a recession every 8.8 years, I believe it is necessary to have a guaranteed income stream for life to cover these essential expenses in your lowest yet most important tier of your financial hierarchy of needs.

How can you best accomplish this? Social Security is certainly a good start, but for most people this will only cover a portion of their Core Expenses. That was the case with John and Mary, whose annual core expenses are $100,000. They receive annual Social Security payments of $35,000, guaranteeing 35 percent of these expenses. Although the baby boomer population may be the last generation in our country to receive company pensions, John and Mary are fortunate to receive an annual pension of $20,000. So between social security and pension, $55,000 or 55 percent of their $100,000 of core expenses is guaranteed, leaving $45,000 that is not protected.

$100,000 Total Annual Core Expenses
-$35,000 Social Security Income
$65,000
-$20,000 Pension Income
$45,000 remaining core expense that is NOT guaranteed

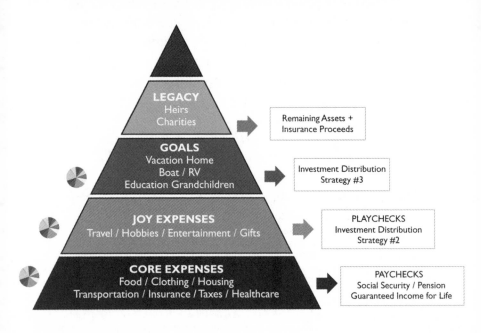

DISTRIBUTION PLANNING
YOUR HIERARCHY OF NEEDS

LEGACY
Heirs
Charities
→ Remaining Assets + Insurance Proceeds

GOALS
Vacation Home
Boat / RV
Education Grandchildren
→ Investment Distribution Strategy #3

JOY EXPENSES
Travel / Hobbies / Entertainment / Gifts
→ PLAYCHECKS Investment Distribution Strategy #2

CORE EXPENSES
Food / Clothing / Housing
Transportation / Insurance / Taxes / Healthcare
→ PAYCHECKS Social Security / Pension Guaranteed Income for Life

Today there are proven strategies offered by the world's largest and highest-rated financial companies that enable you to insure an income stream for life. John and Mary reinvested that final portion of their portfolio into such an approach that now provides them with a guaranteed annual paycheck of $45,000, enough to cover their remaining core expenditures. It has been extremely satisfying for me to observe the peace of mind they now have knowing their essential expenses are covered for life no matter how long they may live and no matter what happens to the stock or real estate markets in the future.

TIER 2: JOY EXPENSES

John and Mary didn't work diligently for so many years just so they could comfortably cover the essential expenses in their retirement years. Like you, they also want to have fun and enjoy these extraordinary years. Moving up their financial hierarchy, the next level is what I call their JOY EXPENSES. These expenses consist of travel, hobbies, entertainment and gifts for grandchildren. I have heard clients make statements such as: "My kids have traveled to Europe for months at a time and we have always worked too hard and have never even been there." John and Mary love international travel including cruises and trips to Europe and the Far East. They are very active and passionate about tennis, golf, and skiing. They have an appreciation for good food and take delight in eating out at fine restaurants. After completing their comprehensive financial plan, we had a good idea how much they anticipated spending on these pleasurable expenditures. I allocated the portion of their assets into a conservative wealth preservation portfolio to provide them with a monthly playcheck to cover the expenses for these gratifying activities.

TIER 3: GOAL EXPENSES

Once John and Mary had a wealth distribution strategy in place that would provide a guaranteed monthly paycheck to cover their core expenses and another diversified investment strategy to provide a monthly playcheck for the fun and adventure in their lives, they were already feeling a sense of levity as weight fell from their shoulders. Some clients are more than content to stop at this level since their core and joy expenses have been taken care of. For others, like John and Mary, who have additional financial objectives and wishes, we look to the next tier of their hierarchy of needs: GOALS. One of my business mentors, Robert Berman, lives by the adage, "A goal without a plan is nothing but a wish." Setting goals in your life and for your years of financial independence has the power to change the course of your life. The father of motivation, Earl Nightingale, coined the phrase: "We become what we think about." These powerful quotes have been so influential in my life that they adorn the walls in my office.

Research proves how critical setting and writing down our goals is if we ever want to reach them. We each have incredible power if only we would take the small amount of time and effort to think out and commit to recording what we want to see happening in our lives.

That's why I always help my clients spell out their financial goals on paper. Clients have different grand visions, from a vacation home on the coast to traveling the continent in a luxurious new motorhome. These goals make up the next level of our hierarchy, and typically have a different time frame and purpose than the previous tiers.

After determining through John and Mary's financial blueprint that they have the highest probability of covering their Core, Joy and Goal Expenses without outliving their income, we invested a portion of their portfolio for this tier and appropriately positioned it with a different investment company with a different heartbeat and purpose to provide for their goals.

All of the investment strategies used for core, joy and goal expenses have a few things in common. As I'll discuss in the next chapter, they are diversified among all of the major asset classes and rebalanced on a regular basis. This is illustrated by the pie chart to the left of each tier on the hierarchy graphic.

TIER 4: APPROACHING THE SUMMIT—LEGACY

Just as with Maslow's hierarchy where the lowest levels of the mountain are made up of the most basic needs, as you move further up your financial hierarchy of needs, the needs become more complex. Once you have fulfilled the first three needs of Core, Joy and Goals, one level at a time, you are prepared to focus on Legacy. This is the bequest you would like to leave behind for your loved ones and it means different things to different people. John and Mary have the desire to cover the expenses of their four grandchildren's college education. Is there a better legacy one could leave behind?

A true plan can offer the benefit of having a remote control from heaven. When properly prepared for, your legacy or estate plan (which we'll talk more about in Chapter 10) should exemplify exactly what your intentions are for the transfer of your wealth upon your passing. Your legacy doesn't just have to mean the transfer of your wealth in the most efficient way. It could mean protecting and enhancing the lives of your loved ones as well as ensuring that your family makes educated financial decisions by learning sound financial principles.

THE SUMMIT: SELF-ACTUALIZATION

The top of the mountain is where self-actualization occurs. This is when you reach a state of harmony and understanding because you are engaged in achieving your full potential and have already satisfied your basic emotional and financial needs. When you receive guaranteed paychecks each month for the remainder of your life to cover your Core Expenses no matter what happens to the markets, you are ready to focus on the next level of Joy. Having a diversified and conservative portfolio provide monthly *playchecks* for your Joy Expenses enables you to focus on the Goal Expenses. Once this is achieved, the focus can move to Legacy. In my experience, when all four levels have been appropriately planned for, my clients reach financial self-actualization. This leads to a lifetime accentuated by a certain calming and peace of mind that is truly priceless. But unless you have a true distribution blueprint in place and have a hierarchy created for your retirement years, you likely won't get there on your own. With the creation of your very own hierarchy of needs, you too can be self-actualized in your years of financial independence.

John recently stopped by my office, unannounced, after returning from Europe. In a high-spirited manner he strolled over to me and gave me a high five followed by an embrace. With great appreciation, he shared that he and Mary had not only flown first class for the first time in five years but, for the first time ever, he had vacationed overseas without ever thinking or worrying about his finances. John and Mary have truly achieved financial self-actualization!

Chapter 8

MAKING THE SOLUTION WORK FOR YOU:
THE CHANGING FACE OF INVESTING

The pessimist complains about the wind.
The optimist expects it to change. The leader adjusts the sails.

—John Maxwell

To achieve financial self-actualization, you need to understand your investment options. If you're clear about those options, you can make solid decisions. If you're not, you can't possibly come up with a financial strategy that is going to serve you well.

A few years ago, I spent a day mountain-biking the 26-mile McKenzie River Trail. Located in Oregon's spectacular Cascade Mountains, the trail traverses lush 300-year-old growth forests, lava fields, and alongside lakes so clean you can see more than 100 feet to the bottom. This lush landscape reminds me of New Zealand. The forest floor is carpeted in an emerald green of thick moss and ferns. The McKenzie River crashes 140 feet over a lava cliff to form the stunning Sahalie Falls. After spending time here, it's easy to see why Bike Magazine gave the McKenzie River Trail its prized No. 1 spot for best trail in America.

Five friends joined me for this exploit. They are all successful professionals in their 50s who have worked hard and accomplished much in their fields of endeavor. Over this enjoyable daylong excursion through the woods, retirement planning somehow became a topic of deep conversation. One of the guys shared that he and his wife had a goal to retire on 1/1/11. He then explained in a heartrending tone how their retirement dream has withered away. Like millions of successful baby boomers they had been blindsided by the financial collapse. I couldn't help but wonder how much better off he and his wife would be today had they been cognizant of the eight key risks of retirement.

It is time to rethink our priorities and get back on track to retirement. While there is no magic pill to get back on the road to financial independence, there are some strategies that can certainly help.

When I begin working with new clients, I am baffled that the majority of these investors have very little in their portfolios to potentially combat the underperformance of their more traditional investments. Wise investors know that a diversified stock portfolio helps cushion against the ups and downs of the market. There are many different groupings of stocks— by industry, by market cap size (large, medium, and small), by investment style (growth, value, and blended), by country (U.S., international), and so forth. These groupings remind me of my son and daughter, who come from the same parents and yet are so very different from each other. Similarly, each of these different types of investments performs in different ways. Often some segments of the investment universe will be rising while others will be falling. Deciding on an appropriate asset mix for your particular situation is critical.

ASSET ALLOCATION

Asset allocation is an investment strategy that attempts to balance risk versus reward by adjusting the percentage of each asset in an investment portfolio according to the investors' risk tolerance, goals, and investment time horizons. Stocks and bonds can often yield wide-ranging results, so investing in a mix of stock and bond funds can improve the performance of your overall portfolio, cushioning your savings against price swings in one asset class.

In terms of return, a diversified portfolio containing both stocks and bonds will generally perform better than either an all-stock or all-bond portfolio over a full market cycle. During the bull market of 1992-1997, a diversified portfolio achieved higher returns than an all-bond portfolio. During the bear market of 1997-2002, the diversified portfolio outperformed the all-stock portfolio.

CHANGING TIMES REQUIRE CHANGING MINDSETS

Asset allocation is one of the most crucial aspects of building a diversified and sustainable portfolio that not only preserves and grows wealth, but also weathers the twists and turns that ever-changing market conditions can throw at it. Indeed, asset allocation has been described as the only free lunch you will find in the investment game because in the past it was as close to a sure thing for long-term investment success. That ceased to work, however, during the crash in 2008. Many investors who thought they were well positioned to manage risk and preserve wealth by going beyond just stocks to invest in bonds, commodities, real estate, international equities and emerging markets suddenly had to scramble because they hadn't anticipated what actually happened. In a year when the S&P 500 lost 37 percent, the MSCI index of major markets in Europe, Asia and Australia lost 45 percent. The MSCI emerging-markets index fell 55 percent. Real-estate investment trusts (REITs) declined 37 percent, high-yield bonds lost 26 percent and commodities fell 37 percent.

When you consider the series of economic and political events that we have never quite experienced concurrently, you realize that there really is no such thing as a free lunch in the investment world. Is Modern Portfolio Theory and Asset Allocation enough? In today's new world economy the answer is a resounding NO! Since *failure is not an option*, it is essential these days to take asset allocation to another level, which I call Strategy Allocation.

In addition to diversifying among the major asset classes, I believe it is important to be diversified among a number of different investment strategies. Strategy Allocation works in sync with the creation of your personal hierarchy of needs discussed in the previous chapter, where your retirement savings is allocated into different tiers. After the impossible became a reality in 2008, when so many of the world's largest financial, investment, banking, and insurance companies declared bankruptcy or vanished, I feel it is vital to have each tier of your portfolio invested with a different purpose, into a different investment strategy, with a different A-rated investment company with the intention of solving a different challenge or accomplishing a different goal. Diversification among financial institutions is not only prudent in today's world, it's essential.

In short, you don't want to abandon asset allocation, but rather to take it to the next level with strategy allocation.

THE RULES FOR WEALTH DISTRIBUTION
HAVE CHANGED

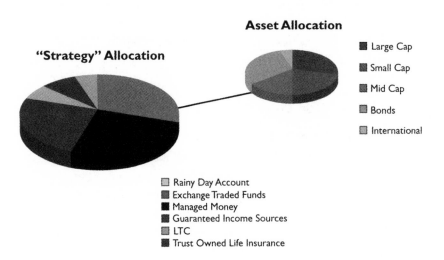

There seem to be endless investment strategies available today. I find that while many people have preconceived notions about different types of investments, they are often misguided and do not have a true understanding of how these investments work. Many ask me what types of investments are best. I answer: "For whom? Under what circumstances? For what portion of your portfolio? What are your time horizons, risk tolerances and liquidity needs?"

In the end, there is no one best investment strategy out there. Each has different pros, cons, fees, terms, and requisites. Your financial advisor should have the universe of financial and insurance tools in his or her quiver so that no matter what your unique situation is, a combination of tactics can be brought together to create an effective Strategy Allocation. It's not my intention to try and educate you about the myriad of investments available today. There are, however, a few significant ones that are often misconstrued and that you should be aware of including Exchange Traded Funds, alternative investments, and Variable Annuities. We'll take them one at a time, but first I want to tell you a story.

WE MAKE OUR OWN OPPORTUNITIES

It was 2008, and the height of apprehension and volatility in the markets. The stock market was about to experience its worst year in history just as home values were plummeting to 50 percent of their value from just a year earlier. We all know people who have worked very hard and accomplished a great deal in their lifetime who proceeded to lose homes and businesses. As I drove through downtown Bend on the way to my office on a bitter February morning, I realized that two very popular restaurants had been bordered up overnight. I later learned that the owners had actually fled town.

People were certainly reacting to the economic woes in different ways. Sadly, a number of successful people I knew of in our community took their own lives. Deeming their circumstances to be hopeless, they despondently made a permanent decision to deal with a temporary problem.

We all have a different relationship to money and prioritize it differently in our lives. I have come to recognize that if people associate their worth as a person to the money they have and they lose that money, they also lose their entire identity or reason for being. I didn't want that to happen to my clients, my firm or me.

Weeks earlier, my team and I had discussed the timeless concept that businesses are either growing or fading. We also recognized that only we as individuals could create the destiny for our own lives. If it is to be, it is up to me! So we made a conscious decision to focus on opportunities and block out any potential fear of failure.

Upon arriving at my office that day, I read the headlines on the front page of my local newspaper stating that the State of Oregon was looking to replace the Wall Street money manager of its Oregon 529 College Plan. The fund had lost over 50 percent of its value even though it had been constructed to never experience such losses. At our morning staff meeting I thought to myself: *Rosell Wealth Management takes advantage of the world's longest (and seriously impressive) track record of managed ETFs. Why don't we vie to be the new manager of the college fund?*

At one time, I would have only daydreamed of investing for such an enormous portfolio. But why not? So despite the fact that we knew we'd be up against big guns like TIAA-CREF, Vanguard, and Fidelity, we went for it. Over the next few weeks, tapping our newly refocused determination, we worked diligently to submit our proposal to the state. We had the belief that we could actually make this a reality. As part of our creative visualization we even had a new college logo developed. It took an additional few months to complete necessary requirements and have our portfolio audited, but it paid off. I will never forget the morning a friend from Portland called to congratulate me for being on the front page of *The Oregonian,* Portland's newspaper.

"What are you talking about?" I asked.

"Rosell Wealth Management made the short list of investment firms from around the country being considered to manage the $500,000,000 Oregon college savings plan!"

Napoleon Hill stated: *Whatever the mind can conceive and believe it can achieve.* We are now believers! How did a small boutique financial firm from Bend, Oregon, get so far? I believe it is because we proposed investing the Oregon 529 College Plan into one of the most advantageous investment vehicles of our generation: Exchange Traded Funds (ETFs).

THE ETF OPPORTUNITY

Have you ever purchased a new car that you think is different and that will stand out? As you are driving home, you suddenly notice that there are a lot of other cars just like it on the road and yours is no longer special. From then on, you see the same car everywhere! Your Reticular Activator—the part of the brain that makes you notice things that you may have otherwise disregarded in the past—has been fired up. That's about to happen to you. Not because you're going to buy a car, but because I'm about to introduce you to an investment strategy that a surprisingly large number of investors have not heard about. Once you finish reading this section, you'll be amazed that you didn't know about Exchange Traded Funds (ETFs) before, since you will begin to see them in television commercials, on billboards, and in print media.

Just as digital downloads have revolutionized music and book publishing, Exchange Traded Funds are changing the way people are investing here in the United States and around the world. ETFs, which are experiencing remarkable growth, have developed into a market worth over $1.75 trillion. Sales of equity ETFs last year hit $122 billion, against outflows of $33 billion from equity mutual funds, according to data provider Morningstar.

At their most basic, ETFs are investment funds listed and traded on a stock exchange that holds assets such as stocks, commodities, or bonds. They are designed to mirror a market index. With over 1,500 different ETFs offered, there is one for practically every index available. In fact, ETFs track nearly twice as many broad-based market indices as traditional index mutual funds. This allows amazing flexibility when it comes to structuring an overall portfolio to the specific needs of any investor. Mutual funds were an incredible idea when they were founded in 1940, back when it was hard for individual investors to build their own stock portfolios. Like many good ideas, they had their day. Today, however, ETFs' qualities have made this one of the fastest-growing investment strategies among financial institutions and individual investors.

An ETF looks like a mutual fund but has important distinctions. ETFs uniquely combine the benefits of stocks and mutual funds into one seamless vehicle, providing advantages that appeal to investors far and wide. The graphic below illustrates the benefits offered by individual stocks as well as mutual funds. ETFs are the sweet spot in the middle where these investments overlap, thereby offering the best of both.

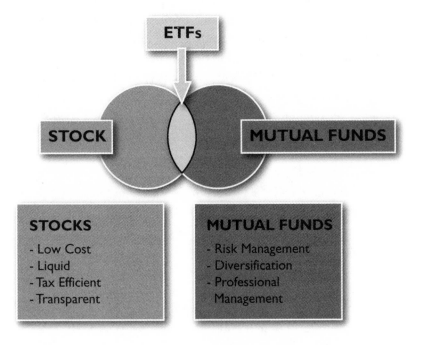

Whether you are a traditional buy-and-hold investor or actively trade to profit from shorter-term opportunities, here are some reasons why you might want to consider ETFs.

- **A Passive Approach to Investing**—ETFs are designed to track an underlying index, such as the S&P 500. While investors have historically relied upon actively managed mutual funds to achieve diversification and asset allocation, most actively managed mutual funds have underperformed market indices over time. An annual study by Standard & Poor's "S&P Indices Vs. Active Funds Scorecard" recently shared that a majority of equity funds were outperformed by their respective index or benchmark over the last one-, three- and five-year periods. It also showed that up to 80 percent of the more expensive actively managed mutual funds fail to beat their benchmark. That's why I believe that actively managed mutual funds have failed to earn their high management fees and have lost ground to ETFs.

- **Low Cost**—Speaking of high fees, helping investors save money is one of the key reasons ETFs really shine since it's not what you make but what you keep that counts. ETFs are no-load funds where you won't be hit with a redemption fee when it's time to liquidate your position. I use ETFs extensively in my clients' accounts because of this investment option's flexibility and low cost. ETFs also typically have lower marketing, distribution, and accounting expenses. The average mutual fund has a net expense ratio of 1.35 percent compared to the average ETF expense ratio of .52 percent. As a result, ETFs may enable you to keep more of what you earn.

- **Tax Efficiency**—Due to the unique features of ETFs, they have become one of the most tax-efficient pooled investment vehicles for investors. Historically, only a few ETFs have ever passed on taxable capital gains distributions to investors. This can make an enormous difference in a non-qualified (non IRA) account. ETFs tend to generate relatively low capital gains, because they typically have low turnover of their portfolio securities. While this is an advantage they share with other index funds, their tax efficiency is further enhanced because they do not have to sell securities to meet investor redemptions. This tax efficiency, along with the reduced costs, can have a positive effect on your overall returns.

• **Liquidity**—Exchange Traded Funds provide the diversification benefits of a mutual fund with the advantage of being traded like an individual stock. Whereas a mutual fund can only be bought or sold based on that day's closing price—calculated after the markets have closed—ETFs can be bought or sold any time throughout the trading day. This allows you to more quickly enter or exit the market during the day. Mutual funds must maintain a certain amount of cash in their portfolio at all times to allow for redemption of shares by investors. ETFs are traded on an exchange and do not require this large cash cushion. This allows investors to be almost fully invested at all times.

• **Transparency**—ETFs are fully transparent investments. The underlying holdings of each ETF are published daily by ETF providers. Compare that to the relatively limited disclosure from mutual funds, which reveal their portfolio holdings after a 60-day lag. Then consider that the average mutual fund replaces its entire portfolio over the course of a year, meaning that at any time you probably don't know what you are actually invested in. Investors know exactly what they own when they purchase an ETF.

- **Diversification and Risk Management**—You already know the drill on diversification: The more securities you own in an asset class, the more protected you may be when any one of those securities takes a nosedive. ETFs are designed to track an index that represents an individual asset class such as large cap, international, bonds, etc. With a single trade, an ETF lets you achieve instant index-like diversification. As I've mentioned, there are ETFs to cover every major index, asset class, and niche an investor can imagine. An entire portfolio of diversified investments can be created quickly and simply by using ETFs. They even offer direct exposure to assets like currencies, real estate and natural resources such as oil and gold. In fact, the easiest way to own gold is through a Gold ETF. This fund will purchase a large amount of gold, maintaining the physical metal in storage. If the price of gold goes up by 10 percent, then individual shares increase in value by the same 10 percent. ETFs can also be used to increase specific exposure of an overall portfolio. For instance, if you want international exposure and also desire to own a greater amount of Japan, you can easily accomplish this by purchasing a broad-based international ETF and a Japan-focused ETF. There are even ETFs designed for growth and others designed for income. ETFs expand diversification and ultimately lower risk while offering opportunities for increased returns.

ETFs are reshaping the way people are investing for their financial future. They offer a combination of benefits that are found in no other investment strategy. As such, they can be an effective way to round out your portfolio. I believe they deserve a serious look to see where they might play a role in your retirement accounts.

BE ALTERNATIVE

Asset allocation is usually assumed to be a mix of the three main asset classes: stocks, bonds, and cash. Many investors believe that a broad mix of equities (financials, health care, utilities and telecoms), an exposure to foreign stocks, and some emerging market plays, some bonds and a foundation of cash, equals diversification. As we've seen, however, this traditional approach is outdated. It also completely excludes several key asset classes I'll describe below. Many asset classes are positively correlated. A portfolio that consists entirely of positively correlated asset classes cannot achieve optimal diversification.

When it comes to investing, many people have been asking themselves "What am I doing wrong?" or possibly the more optimistic "What could I be doing better?" During such volatile and erratic times, it is only logical for people to question traditional investing methods. So let's look at those investors who have actually grown their assets in the face of this unprecedented volatility by stepping away from traditional investing. These investors share an investment strategy based on two guiding principles. First, they recognize that avoiding large losses is more important than trying to earn large gains. Second, they understand the need to generate enough income to provide the money needed without eating into the principal investment.

Who are these success stories? They are institutional investors—pensions and endowments such as Ivy League schools. Where are these institutional investors putting their money? They are diversifying a part of their portfolios into alternative investments.

Now you are probably asking yourself, what are alternative investments? They can easily be explained as anything outside of traditional stocks, bonds, and cash. Alternative investments include asset classes like commodities that come out of the earth in the form of raw materials, agricultural goods, and oil, along with real estate and more sophisticated asset classes such as hedge funds, managed futures, and derivatives. And these alternative investments are now available to you.

Today's economic challenges have created a demand for this new thinking. As a result, wealth advisors now have the ability to provide you with investment opportunities that replicate the strategies and investment goals of those larger institutions that actually made money during The Lost Decade. Alternative investments did better than so many other investments during that time because they have a low correlation with a majority of typical asset classes. Let me explain. Two investments that have different risk/return characteristics and behave differently in response to market events would likely show little similarity in returns over time, thereby exhibiting a low correlation. Investments that are not well correlated to one another will help lower the overall volatility of the portfolio, even if the underlying investment itself is volatile. When one asset goes down, other assets will go up. That's why top wealth advisors have increasingly sought out low correlation alternative asset classes. Adding such investments into the equation has proven to improve returns while decreasing risk.

When the average annual return of the S&P 500 had a return of -1.6 percent over the previous decade, the returns of the 460 largest endowments were in positive territory over that same period, ranging from a 5 percent average annual return for the large endowments to lower, but still positive, returns for smaller endowments.

Typically, investors look for growth in U.S. equities. Remarkably, when we examine the top three performing asset classes over a ten-year period, U.S. equities never made the top three. In fact, traditional asset classes altogether only made the cut a total of three times out of 30. In other words, 90 percent of the time, alternative portfolios dominated the top three performing asset classes. The endowments, big institutions, foundations, and pensions have known this for decades, and so they marry traditional investments with alternatives in an attempt to adjust their portfolio's risk/return characteristics. By constructing portfolios with allocations to both traditional and alternative assets, institutional investors seek to reduce expected risks while improving the potential for greater returns.

Until recently most alternative investments were only held by institutions or very high net-worth individuals due to very high investment minimums, stringent regulations and their inherent complexity. Today it is not only possible but also rather easy for average investors saving for, or already in, retirement to have a portion of their portfolio invested into these alternative investments. Past performance would indicate that this is an idea worth considering. So is the notion of actually insuring a portion of your investments.

ALTERNATIVES AND PERFORMANCE

2002	2003	2004	2005	2006	2007	2008	2009	2010	2011
Commodities 25.91%	Emerging Market Equities 56.28%	Real Estate 37.84%	Emerging Market Equities 34.54%	Real Estate 42.35%	Emerging Market Equities 39.78%	Managed Futures 18.28%	Emerging Market Equities 79.02%	Private Equity 31.50%	Global Infrastructure 13.75%
Managed Futures 18.83%	Real Estate 40.69%	Global Infrastructure 32.81%	Commodities 21.36%	Global Infrastructure 36.65%	Global Infrastructure 16.26%	Bonds 5.23%	Private Equity 61.65%	Real Estate 20.04%	Bonds 7.84%
Emerging Market Bond 13.65%	International Equity 39.17%	Private Equity 27.98%	Private Equity 17.58%	Emerging Market Equity 32.59%	Commodities 16.23%	Emerging Market Bonds -12.00%	Real Estate 38.26%	Emerging Market Equities 19.20%	Emerging Market Bonds 7.35%
Bonds 10.25%	US Equities 31.06%	Emerging Market Equity 25.87%	Real Estate 15.35%	International Equity 26.86%	Hedge Funds 12.56%	Hedge Funds -19.03%	Global Infrastructure 34.24%	US Equities 16.93%	US Equities 1.03%
Hedge Funds 3.04%	Global Infrastructure 28.98%	International Equity 20.64%	International Equity 14.02%	Private Equity 26.81%	International Equity 11.63%	Commodities -35%.57	International Equity 32.46%	Commodities 16.83%	Hedge Funds -2.31%
Real Estate 2.82%	Commodities 23.93%	US Equities 11.91%	Global Infrastructure 11.01%	US Equities 15.72%	Bonds 6.97%	Global Infrastructure -36.28%	Emerging Market Bonds 29.81%	Global Infrastructure 12.46%	Managed Futures -4.94%
Emerging Market Equity -6.00%	Emerging Market Bonds 22.21%	Emerging Market Bonds 11.58%	Emerging Market Bonds 10.25%	Hedge Funds 13.86%	Emerging Market Bonds 6.16%	US Equities -37.23%	US Equities 28.34%	Emerging Market Bonds 12.24%	Real Estate -5.82%
International Equity -15.66%	Hedge Funds 15.44%	Hedge Funds 9.61%	Hedge Funds 7.61%	Emerging Market Bonds 9.86%	Managed Futures 6.01%	International Equity -42.97%	Commodities 18.91%	Managed Futures 12.22%	International Equity -11.73%
US Equities -21.54%	Managed Futures 14.13	Commodities 9.12%	US Equities 6.12%	Managed Futures 8.05%	US Equities 5.14%	Real Estate -47.63%	Hedge Funds 18.57%	Hedge Funds 10.95%	Commodities -13.32%
	Bonds 4.10%	Managed Futures 5.95%	Bonds 2.43%	Bonds 4.33%	Real Estate -6.96%	Emerging Market Equity -53.08%	Bonds 5.93%	International Equity 8.21%	Emerging Market Equity -18.7%
		Bonds 4.33%	Managed Futures -0.11%	Commodities 2.07%	Private Equity -10.37%	Private Equity -64.05%	Managed Futures -6.57%	Bonds 6.54%	Private Equity -18.85%

PORTFOLIO INSURANCE

Given that it is essentially impossible to time the markets and that retirees can't afford to partake in significant market losses, wouldn't it be great if there was another option where you didn't have to worry about when to get in or get out?

Wouldn't it be valuable if there were an investment strategy that enabled you to stay invested in the market while providing guarantees that you would have an income stream for life regardless of market performance?

These benefits are now available. When used appropriately, for the right people, for the right portion of a portfolio, and at the right time in your life, they can offer noteworthy benefits and save that retirement income you've worked most of your life to accumulate.

If you're like most people, you probably insure your most valuable assets. This typically includes your home, cars, boat, jewelry, and even your own life. During your working years, you may have owned disability insurance to insure your ability to earn an income. Now it is possible to insure what for most people at or near retirement is their most valuable financial asset: their retirement accounts.

The word annuity historically has been associated with disapproval. Why is this? Before I answer that, let's review what annuities are. Think of an annuity as the opposite of life insurance. Life insurance is meant to protect loved ones should you die prematurely. Annuities are there to protect you should you outlive your retirement savings. In the past Mom and Dad would give an insurance company a sum of money in return for an income stream for life. If they lived a long time they came out ahead of the game and families were pleased. If they died the next day, the insurance company kept the rest of the money. These families understandably felt ripped off.

Today, the modern-day Variable Annuity (VA) with living benefits offers a different and more cheerful story. In July 2009 *The Wall Street Journal* ran a story titled "Long Derided This Investment Now Looks Wise—Thanks to Guarantees, Variable Annuities Paid When Stock Didn't." The headline says it all. Variable Annuities can ease investors' anxieties and lead to better investment outcomes. They help investors avoid common behavioral pitfalls such as attempts at market timing while maintaining the market exposure needed for long-term investment success. These advantages have never been more apparent than during the current period of extreme volatility.

The decision for retired investors about whether to get out or stay in the market is of the utmost importance. However, if they elect to put the money into a VA with a living benefit, this decision is no longer an issue. They are still invested into the market as the investments inside of many VAs offer mutual funds and ETFs. Some even offer alternative investments. However, their performance downside is now protected because these VA investors have guaranteed lifetime income throughout their retirement.

Let's suppose you have $1,000,000 invested in a retirement account. If you choose a 5 percent living benefit, you are guaranteed $50,000 a year in retirement. Even if the markets were to crash and your $1,000,000 account value dropped to $500,000, you could still withdraw $50,000 a year because of the guarantees. Eventually the withdrawals can reduce the contract value to zero, but even here with a zero balance, you will receive $50,000 annually (net of all fees) for the rest of your life.

It gets even more advantageous. As the contract owner, you are protected from downside market performance as stated above and yet still have room for growth on the upside. Suppose, for example, that the market does well and the value of the contract rises to $1,200,000. This is now the guaranteed amount off of which the living benefit is calculated. With a 5 percent payout, that would equate to $60,000 annually.

Such an investment strategy can mitigate our worst knee-jerk reactions, which we'll talk about in Chapter 12, as well as underperforming markets, and offer investors the guarantees and psychological support needed to maintain market exposure. VAs, like any investment strategy, should be only part of the retirement security puzzle. But it's an important part that should not be overlooked. At the very least retirees should consider VAs with living benefits for a portion of their portfolio. This is an appropriate addition to Social Security and other pensions you may have to cover your core expenses when creating your financial hierarchy of needs. By adding VAs to the mix, you are able to create a personal pension for yourself that provides guaranteed income for life. There are not too many other ways to accomplish this.

Of course, guarantees are only as strong as the company behind them, so I suggest only using A+-rated insurance companies. Keep in mind that there is an additional cost to insure your income stream for life, but the guaranteed withdrawals are net of fees. With any added benefit, *costs only become an issue in the absence of value.* There is no greater value than peace of mind when it comes to your investments, especially during your retirement years.

Chapter 9

THE TOUGHER YOU ARE ON YOURSELF
TODAY, THE EASIER LIFE WILL BE LATER ON

The future belongs to those
who believe in the beauty of their dreams.

—Bart Forbes

Whether you're climbing toward retirement or have reached that summit, the financial principles that help you attain financial independence will be the same principles that allow you to not outlive your money. I have my grandmother to thank for instilling that notion in me so early on.

My Grandma Ruth knew that passing along her practical lessons to me would spark my interest and passion for personal finance and set me up for life. So she instilled in me some essential philosophies that still resonate with me today:

- One doesn't need to do anything extraordinary to accumulate wealth over time. One just needs to do some ordinary things extraordinarily well.
- Saving 10 percent of your income is not remarkable. Doing so over every pay period for 40 years is.
- The tougher I am on myself today, the easier life will be on me later.

Unfortunately, most people haven't had someone like my Grandma Ruth to guide them on the money front. And so they make big, expensive mistakes that negatively impact their bottom line as well as their future financial well-being.

Why is personal finance so hard for most people? I believe we are hardwired to make financial mistakes because most of our financial lessons have come from our parents. Parents help cultivate whatever aptitudes we have. I know my mom and dad did that for me. Through their unconditional love, our parents give us the confidence to face the world. But when it comes right down to it, what do most of them know about personal finance? Where did they learn their all too often poor money habits? From *their* parents, who more than likely were raised during the Great Depression. Often their association to money is that of fear, lack, and despair. Who would want to learn financial lessons from someone with these experiences? The other major source of financial education comes from the constant barrage of so-called experts on 24-hour television news who are well aware that fear sells.

WHAT'S THE PROBLEM?

Financial failure may not be an option, but apparently plenty of folks haven't gotten that memo. The statistics are startling. According to Pew Research, a full 42 percent of American families make less money than they spend. It is easy to see why personal bankruptcies have skyrocketed. Historically our schools have not taught anything practical about money. According to "Teach Kids About Money by Igniting Their Entrepreneurial Spirit!" in *Success for Women* magazine, only 34 percent of teens understand credit card fees. Universities are often filled with solicitors offering credit cards to students turning 18. As one can easily imagine, these young shoppers who do not understand credit card interest respond to being bombarded with the latest must haves by maxing out their credit cards.

Could our recent economic crisis have been prevented if a few simple lessons in money management and personal finance had been taught in our schools over the past few decades? Money can be so hard to make but so easy to spend. Wouldn't it be great to have a modern-day piggy bank with four chambers—one for saving, one for spending, one for donating, and one for investing?

FINANCIALLY SAVVY KIDS

One of the answers to a brighter financial future for our nation is to have financially savvy kids. Schools should teach our kids the lessons of financial responsibility we were never exposed to in K-12—or even college, for that matter. It is never too early to start learning about money. It amazes me that we teach even our young children how to go out and work for a living, but not about what to do with the money once they've earned it. As they get older, they learn about politics, history, and family planning, but never about financial responsibility. Shouldn't there be a prerequisite course on personal finance before one graduates high school, college, or graduate school? Universities know that the average graduate will make millions of dollars during his or her career and yet there is no required course on the basic principles of money management.

Personal finance should be as important as reading, writing, and arithmetic in our schools.

Grandma Ruth preached that rather than teach complicated investment strategies, we should offer a back-to-the-basics approach to handling money:

- Don't spend what you don't have.
- Save a portion of every dollar that you earn and invest in the stock market for long-term rather than short-term gains.

It's time for all of us to get schooled about money, and for us to financially prepare our offspring for their adult lives. If your children's or grandchildren's school will not teach these lessons, it is important that we as parents and grandparents do. Our kids should be encouraged to open up savings accounts rather than credit cards. They need to become knowledgeable about personal budgets, investing for their future, compound interest, and the Law of 72.

THE POWER OF COMPOUND INTEREST

The great Albert Einstein published more than 300 scientific papers and developed endless formulas including the theory of relativity. In 1921 he received the Nobel Prize in physics. His great intelligence has made the word *Einstein* synonymous with genius. What I find most interesting is that with all of the theories, formulas, and principles he developed, he is reputed to have said: *The most powerful force in the universe is that of compound interest.*

This concept is incredibly important when it comes to planning your financial future. Compound interest ensues when interest is added to the principal; from that moment on, the interest that has been added also earns interest.

Grandma once asked me if I were given a choice to receive one million dollars in one month or a penny doubled every day for 30 days, which I would choose. Without hesitating, I chose the million dollars. She went on to share the alternative:

Day 1: $ .01	**Day 7:** $ .64	**Day 13:** $ 40.96	**Day 19:** $ 2,621	**Day 25:** $ 167,772
Day 2: $ .02	**Day 8:** $ 1.28	**Day 14:** $ 81.92	**Day 20:** $ 5,232	**Day 26:** $ 335,544
Day 3: $ .04	**Day 9:** $ 2.56	**Day 15:** $ 163.84	**Day 21:** $ 10,485	**Day 27:** $ 671,088
Day 4: $ .08	**Day 10:** $ 5.12	**Day 16:** $ 327.68	**Day 22:** $ 20,971	**Day 28:** $ 1,342,177
Day 5: $ .16	**Day 11:** $ 10.24	**Day 17:** $ 655.36	**Day 23:** $ 41,943	**Day 29:** $ 2,684,354
Day 6: $ .32	**Day 12:** $ 20.48	**Day 18:** $ 1,310	**Day 24:** $ 83,886	**Day 30:** $ 5,368,709

This chart illustrates the unexpected yet astonishing result of doubling that initial penny every day. After just 30 days, you would wind up with over five million dollars. This is the power of compounding. Note that in the last six days, your assets jump from $167,772 to $5,368,709. That is why it is crucial to start planning and investing early in life. Investing is like a rocket ship taking off into space. It spends 80 percent of its fuel during takeoff and once it reaches a certain point, it flies smoothly with minimal consumption.

Because the benefits of saving early in life are so greatly magnified by compounding, getting started with investing at a young age can make a big difference in how much wealth is ultimately accumulated. And while retirement may have little importance to most teenagers, they just might become interested in the magical powers of compounding. Albert Einstein allegedly called it the Eighth Wonder. "It can work for you, or against you," he is said to have stated. "When you invest it works for you. When you borrow it works against you."

THE LAW OF 72

One of the handiest financial formulas I use, and one that our children could learn to appreciate, is also attributed to Albert Einstein. The Law of 72 is an easy way to approximate how quickly your money will double at a given rate of return. Here's how it works:

Simply divide 72 by the annual rate of return you expect on your investment. Let's say you invest $100,000 in an investment earning a hypothetical 6 percent annually. According to the equation, (72 divided by 6), your investment would double to approximately $200,000 in 12 years. If your real estate portfolio has been earning 8 percent a year, it would only take nine years to double the value of your investment (72 divided by 8).

THE LAW OF 72 CALCULATIONS:

Years to Double Your Money	36 yrs	18 yrs	12 yrs	9 yrs	7.2 yrs	6 yrs
Necessary Investment Return	2%	4%	6%	8%	10%	12%

Sharing the powerful effects of compounding and the Law of 72 can motivate your children or grandchildren to invest early in life, just like I did after Grandma Ruth and my father shared them with me. You never know when you can impress your family and friends by asking them the doubling penny question or by running instant figures in your head regarding how long it takes to double an investment at a particular rate of return.

There are numerous ways to leave a legacy behind for your loved ones. It can be in the form of transferring wealth from one generation to another or, as in the case with Grandma Ruth, through sage financial lessons. What will your legacy be?

Chapter 10

Estate of Confusion

It is tough to make predictions, especially about the future.

—*Yogi Berra*

Wh hen I first meet with clients, they share their financial
goals, hopes, concerns, and fears with me. I find that
most associate money with security or freedom, although the
definition of these words can often have different meanings for
different people. As I help them peel off the layers of the onion to
get to their true desires, nearly everyone seems to have the same
objective: obtaining true financial peace of mind during their retirement years. Many also wish to leave a legacy behind to loved
ones when they pass on. Their intention is to help ensure that
their surviving family members—and sometimes even charities
they care about—also gain financial security and freedom.

Freedom—financial or otherwise—is not just an amorphous
concept. It's a tangible reality that profoundly changes one's life. I
saw that firsthand in 1989 when Mikhail Gorbachev announced
that troops would no longer intervene in the internal affairs
of Soviet Satellite nations. Countries threw off communism in
quick succession and on November 9 the Berlin Wall fell. My

high school friend Eric Johnson and I were there to celebrate and witness history being made in front of our eyes. Just a week later, the Velvet Revolution erupted in Czechoslovakia, and Eric and I beelined to Wenceslas Square in Prague. We were two of over 500,000 people who took to the streets demanding an end to communist rule, chanting: *"Havel, na Hrad! Havel, na Hrad!"* (Havel to the Castle!) We had no idea that this demonstration would lead to the resignation of the communist regime. A few weeks later, the acclaimed playwright Václav Havel, who had spent most his 40s in and out of prison due to his writings, which outspokenly criticized the communist system, would be elected president and would move into the Prague Castle, a significant Czech monument.

Czechoslovakia is free!

During the next few weeks of our journey, we saw Romania, Poland, and Hungary fall from communism. In Romania the 22-year brutal and repressive regime headed by Nicolae Ceauşescu came to an abrupt end as he and his wife, Elena, were executed following a televised two-hour court session. The energy outside the Romanian Embassy in Prague was somber yet triumphant.

From Belgrade, the former capital of Yugoslavia (now Serbia), Eric and I took an overnight train heading for Budapest to help the Hungarians celebrate their newfound freedom. This would not be an ordinary evening or jaunt across the border. It started out by almost missing our train as the solemn woman behind the ticket counter refused to accept U.S. dollars, a problem since we had purposely spent down our dinars. As the train was about to leave the station, she finally took our dollars and gave us two tickets for our seven-hour trip to Szeged. We ran onto the packed train and quickly came to the realization that there were no unoccupied seats for us. Since we were hungry, we decided to deal with the lack of seating after seeking out the dining car. That's when we discovered there wasn't one. We wound up standing in the hallway, and eventually sitting—and then going horizontal—on the dirty floor to try to catch some shut-eye. The international occupants of the train did their best to walk over us on their way to the WC (wash closet/bathroom).

In the middle of the night, as we listened to a group of Russians rejoicing with vodka in their cabin, the train suddenly came to a stop. We had no idea that we had reached the border, which at the time still had a barbed-wire fence that would soon be dismantled. Soldiers wearing Russian Ushanka fur hats boarded the train with their forbidding Kalashnikov assault rifles dating back to WWII. In a hostile tone they asked to see everyone's passports, then proceeded to order Eric and me off the train. We looked at each other in alarm as we were ushered into a cold room at the station. Minutes later Nikky and Eric from Canada, Peter from Australia, Yamoney from Japan, and Johan and René from East Germany joined us from the train. They were just as frightened and confused as we were. None of us had any idea why we were being held or what lay in store.

As the hours passed, we played chess to calm our nerves, talked, and wondered where we would end up. Eric and I tried to stay positive, but having been deprived of our liberty and having gone all day and night without any food made that increasingly difficult. Finally, seven hours later, a soldier advised us that we had not procured the visa necessary to enter Hungary. As a result, we would be placed on the next train back to Subotica, over the Yugoslavian border.

Relief doesn't begin to describe our emotions when we boarded that train. We were free! In Subotica we took a taxi to the police station where, after almost two days with no sleep, photos were taken for our visa. A short train ride later we were back at the border on the Yugoslavian side. In a scene right out of the movies, we walked 100 yards in the dark, snowy night through Passport Control and into Hungary. We were then informed that we had a five-mile walk ahead of us to get to the train station.

A photo of our passports after their return by the soldiers.

Cold and dark, yet comforted by being in a large group of new friends, we began our slog. Minutes later, three men armed with Soviet shotguns emerged from the woods, startling the entire group. I think we all envisioned another incarceration, but they simply waved us on. Luckily, a young man picked us all up in his truck just then and took us to a disco in the middle of what seemed like nowhere but turned out to be adjacent to the train station.

The club was filled with young people, all of whom turned their attention to our international crew. We danced to Phil Collins and partook of their local libations. Somehow I found myself being kissed by a Hungarian girl in a red dress. She knew very little English, but I didn't care. Yamoney, from

Japan, had a video recorder, which freaked out the young Hungarians who had never seen one before. He filmed everyone and then connected the camera to the antiquated television in the disco. The young Hungarians were so excited that they began buying him drinks. Eventually, as a train with CCCP plastered on the outside pulled into the station, I exchanged addresses with the lady in red. Then we said our goodbyes and headed off to Budapest. The unexpectedly joyous end to the whole bizarre experience, however, couldn't erase the feelings of trepidation and helplessness I had experienced while being detained.

Your liberty might not be at stake when it comes to estate planning and your legacy, but everything else you've spent a lifetime building certainly is. The problem is that you're probably just as confused as I was when the guards ordered us off that train and detained us. Fortunately, there are strategies to enable you to transfer your wealth in an efficient manner. It is important to seek expert advice and become familiar with these different methods. Significant changes related to estate tax laws have recently been implemented. My intention in this chapter is to inform you of some of the key modifications, share a few techniques to help ensure that Uncle Sam does not become your No.1 beneficiary, and motivate you to put your estate plan in order.

The most important reason to plan is to make sure that what you want to happen after you're gone actually does. Who gets control of the business? Who gets the family home? Will a special-needs grandchild—or any grandchild, for that matter—have the necessary funds available?

Earlier in this book, we discussed the need for a comprehensive financial plan that encompasses both asset and strategy allocation. Planning out your legacy requires an equally strategic approach. There are numerous ways people share their wealth with others; giving to children, grandchildren and charities are just a few examples. Similarly, there are a myriad of estate planning strategies to help affluent investors reduce or eliminate potential state taxes. In this chapter, I hope to offer you a glimpse of what is possible.

There is a lot of confusion about estate taxes. We are all aware that the current federal debt and deficits have ballooned to record levels over the past dozen years. I believe no matter which political party is in power, taxes will eventually be increased in order to maintain current government services and programs. High-income taxpayers will continue to shoulder the burden in a number of ways. Do not assume that your existing documents will meet all of your goals. Often they won't. Those who adopt a wait-and-see approach may find that they have defaulted to a wait-and-pay approach, which gets us right back to the subject of taxation.

ESTATE TAXES

After years of changes, political arm-twisting, and the indecisiveness of our polarized Congress, the federal estate tax rules have finally become clear and stable. As of 2013, those rules are now set permanently into the tax code—at least until the tax code changes again. The amount an individual can exclude from estate taxes (including gifts given during his or her lifetime) is a generous $5.25 million per person.

That amount means that few people will actually be subject to this tax. After all, with smart estate planning, a couple could exclude $10.5 million from estate or gift taxes.

Transfers in excess of the exemption amount are now subject to tax at a 40 percent rate, up from 35 percent. The Tax Policy Center estimates only 3,800 estates are expected to be big enough to owe any federal estate tax in 2013. The exclusion was scheduled to revert to $1 million per person in 2013 with a 55 percent tax rate on most estates, which made millions of Americans apprehensive. Many of those living in high-priced real estate located in places like San Francisco, New York and Boston would have fallen into the estate tax bracket, since they already had taxable estates worth $1 million before even figuring in their other retirement assets. That prospect prompted wealthy clients to race though plans and gifts that ordinarily might have been handled slowly and thoughtfully. I'm pretty sure that Uncle Sam probably isn't your beneficiary of choice, so if you are one of those who threw together something in great haste, I would urge you to review your estate plan and make sure it reflects your wishes.

ESTATE OF CONFUSION
Will Uncle Sam Become Your #1 Benificiary?

YEAR	EXCLUSION AMOUNT	MAX TAX RATE
2001	$675,000	55%
2002	$1 million	50%
2003	$1 million	49%
2004	$15 million	48%
2005	$15 million	47%
2006	$2 million	46%
2007	$2 million	45%
2008	$2 million	45%
2009	$35 million	45%
2010	----- R E P E A L E D -----	
2011	$5 million	35%
2012	$5.12 million	35%
2013*	$5.25 million	40%

*The American Taxpayer Relief Act of 2012 - enacted on January 2, 2013

Even if you doubt that you'll ever have a taxable estate, it still pays to plan ahead. If you think you don't have to worry about estate taxes because of the new generous federal estate tax law, please note that for many the estate tax unfortunately does not end with the federal government. Separate state levies are still a big concern for families in 21 states and the District of Columbia. In the face of severe budget deficits, some states have implemented estate and inheritance taxes that kick in at lower levels than do the federal ones, which could result in a bite out of funds you had hoped to pass on. As an example, fiscally challenged Oregon where I reside is one of a handful of states that imposes its own estate tax. Under current law, if you are an Oregon resident or own assets located in Oregon, and the combined value of your total estate (wherever it's located) is in excess of $1 million, your estate must file an Oregon estate tax return and pay Oregon estate tax. The tax rate varies between 10 and 16 percent depending on the size of the estate. The tax applies to all of the assets that are in excess of the $1 million deduction. That's not a tough threshold to meet or exceed once you calculate in the value of your home.

In short, you need to pay attention to the rules in your state and think about estate taxes regardless of your level of assets. Keep in mind that you don't have to wait to die before bequeathing money to your beneficiaries. In addition to your lifetime gift tax exemption, in 2013 you may gift $14,000 each year to one or more individuals; a married couple may gift $28,000 to each person. This annual gifting amount is called the gift tax annual exclusion. These gifts don't count toward the lifetime $5.25 million exclusion, and can add up quickly. A couple with two adult married children, for example, could give $28,000 to each this year, plus $28,000 to each spouse, for a total of $56,000. With education costs high and rising, these funds could jumpstart a 529 college savings plan for your grandchildren or help with the down payment of their first home. You can also support a philanthropic goal in this manner.

A WIN FOR YOU, YOUR HEIRS AND THE CHARITIES YOU CARE ABOUT

I have always taught my kids that the more they give, the more that will get in their lives. In this section, I will share an estate planning technique that takes this thought to the next level. When properly structured, it is a win for donors, their heirs, and their charity or charities of choice. In addition to the joy of giving, there are a number of other incentives for charitable contributions that successful people are often not aware of. Some of these diverse objectives may be achieved through a type of tax-exempt trust known as a Charitable Remainder Trust (CRT).

Here are the basics: A donor establishes a CRT by transferring debt-free assets into an irrevocable trust. Once the trustee sells the assets, the proceeds of the sale are invested in an income-producing portfolio. In the case of a married couple, this income can last until the death of the surviving spouse, whereupon the principal of the trust passes to the designated charity or charities. So appreciated stock, real estate, or other appreciated assets can be converted into an income stream that provides retirement income while eventually assisting a worthwhile charitable cause.

In establishing a CRT, the donor receives:
- An income tax deduction for the present value of the trust's remainder interest directed to the charity.
- Lifetime annual income for the donor and spouse.
- The satisfaction of helping a worthy cause, as the principal of the trust is distributed to a designated charity.
- The potential avoidance of capital gains taxes.
- A more diversified investment portfolio.
- The reduction or elimination of potential estate taxes, as the donor's estate is reduced by the assets transferred into the trust.

If you currently own highly appreciated assets—such as stocks or property—and would like to sell the asset but are concerned about paying a large capital gains tax, a CRT allows you to enjoy the benefits of the appreciated assets without having to pay any capital gains taxes. A CRT may offer substantial financial flexibility, even to middle-income bracket taxpayers who have held onto non-income producing assets simply because they don't know about helpful alternatives.

WEALTH REPLACEMENT LIFE INSURANCE

Developing strategies to reduce estate taxes while increasing charitable contributions may be important priorities, but most grantors don't wish to disinherit loved ones. This situation can be addressed by using a portion of the income generated by the CRT to purchase a wealth replacement life insurance policy. The amount of insurance replaces the value of the assets gifted to the CRT, which will eventually pass to your named charities. When properly structured, the proceeds of this policy can be arranged to pass free from both income and estate taxation to the family's children or heirs at the death of the surviving spouse.

Business owners, families, and individuals can benefit from the use of CRTs in achieving charitable as well as financial objectives. CRTs, however, are governed by a complex network of regulations. To ensure both the charitable contribution and full tax benefits, a CRT must be structured by an experienced estate planning team that includes an estate planning attorney, CPA, and a wealth manager with an extensive life insurance background.

The benefits of a CRT are significant. In review, they can reduce your income taxes now, your estate taxes when you die, and allow you to help a charity that's meaningful to you. In other words, you can still reap a benefit from the assets and enjoy the exhilaration of your benevolence, while endowing your selected charity with a sizable gift. Now that's what I call love.

A FINAL ACT OF LOVE

What would your family do if you were suddenly out of the picture? Would anyone know what you owned and where it was located? Would they be able to pay the bills you owe and collect the money due to you? What about important papers—like your will? Is there a record of where you keep it? Do they know the names of your attorney and financial advisor?

Even if you've drawn up the necessary papers to ensure your family's well-being, it is essential to keep records accessible so that whoever is responsible can figure out what to do next. Your executor, attorney, spouse, adult child and/or other reliable party should know where to find your records.

At the time of a loved one's sudden incapacity or death, I have often seen clients overwhelmed by the situation and all the decisions that need to be made, especially in cases where the wishes of the deceased were unknown. Many people have unfortunately experienced such stressful times and witnessed how the strongest of family relationships can be tested and sometimes permanently impaired.

Recognizing that these vital documents—the will, power of attorney, and living will—can be essential components when it comes to making important decisions, Rosell Wealth Management has adopted a program called the Family Love Letter (FLL). Originally written by John Scroggin, the Family Love Letter was designed to provide information in a time of grief, stress, and confusion. We work with individuals to help them gather the information and complete the FLL.

This is not a financial or legal document, but a system to help you organize your finances, thoughts, wishes, and assets. Using simple steps—like making sure all important financial information and other important documents are organized and stored in a fireproof box—the FLL helps bring you the peace of mind you want and need in order to give your family essential information when you can no longer supply it. This financial letter is not intended to replace or supersede other legal documents such as wills or trusts. In fact, you should consult your attorney regarding the validity and enforceability of all your estate planning documents including the FLL. The intention behind the FLL is simply to supplement these documents with potentially helpful information at a difficult time.

Typical information found in a completed FLL includes:
- Where wills and other important papers are kept (do not put in a safe deposit box as your family may need a court order to open it)
- Bank accounts (checking, savings, CDs)
- Investments (stocks, bonds, ETFs, mutual funds, annuities)
- Retirement assets (401(k)s, IRAs, annuities)
- Insurance policies (personal, property)
- Business interests
- Real estate

- Assets held in trust
- Personal property (jewelry, art, collectibles)
- Debts you owe
- Money due to you

No one likes to think about these matters, but by pulling these important documents together and having important details—email passwords, codes to the safe, etc.—in one place, you can get your proverbial house in order for the good of those you care about most. I recommend doing this for the love of your family because you won't be around to make sure they get it right. And you certainly don't want failure to be an option.

Chapter 11

Financial Lessons
From The Road Less Traveled

*If there is to be any peace
it will come through being, not having.*

—Henry Miller

Are you riding the financial train toward success? Our fiscal sensibilities and practices—for better or worse—derive from a multitude of influences and influencers. The key is to surround yourself with positive role models and teachers. As I have already shared, Grandma Ruth and my parents provided me with solid values and a robust financial foundation. But that was just the start. Several others have also dramatically influenced my personal and financial well-being through lessons they shared, lessons I believe you will profit from as well.

One such person entered my life unexpectedly during my senior year in high school thanks to my father, a successful dentist who always had a motivational cassette tape playing in his car. Yes, this was the time period between 8-tracks and CDs. The motivation/self-help craze was in full force. I would always bellow to my dad while in his car: "Dad, would you please just take out that tape and put on the FM radio? PLEASE!" One day we were on a three-hour car ride to see my grandparents in New York City. It could have been the soothing voice, being bored as the fields of the Hudson Valley passed by, or being in a mellow state of mind, but for the first time ever I found myself actually listening to the words from one of Dad's cassettes rather than just hearing them as noise. That's when I heard a message that, despite its simplicity, would shape my entire future.

Dr. Wayne Dyer shared that no matter how much we feel guilty about yesterday it will not change the past. No matter how much we worry about tomorrow, it will not change our future. So live today!

Despite my embarrassment, I asked Dad if I could listen to the rest of the tapes on my new Sony Walkman. From there I started running and exercising to tapes from other Dr. Dyer contemporaries, including Earl Nightingale, Brian Tracy, Zig Ziglar, Denis Waitley, Roger Dawson, and Tony Robbins, on subjects such as personal finance, sales, psychology, neuro-linguistic programming (NLP), motivation, excellence, and living life as an adventure.

When I went off to my freshman year of college, my dad left Dr. Dyer's first book *Erroneous Zones* (not *Erogenous Zones*) on my bed in my dorm. I could not get enough of his message. I read every one of his books, listened to every one of his tapes. By the time I sent Dr. Dyer a letter to tell him how profoundly he had influenced my life, I had started to think of him as Wayne. I still have his response.

On graduation day from college, I wrote *Wayne #1* on my cap. No one knew what it meant, but it was my way of recognizing the person who had already made such an impact on my young life.

Ten years later, in 2000, I moved to Bend, Oregon. The week my wife and I arrived in our beautiful new hometown, Wayne Dyer was speaking live at our local lecture hall. Serendipity once again! I remember Wayne touching Jill's belly after sharing with him that we had just learned our first-born was on the way. Wayne's quotes—including *you will see it when you believe it*—are featured in my brochures and plastered on the wall in my office's reception room. He taught me critical life lessons that shaped me at a young age. Over the last 25 years, those have served me, my clients, and our respective bottom lines. May the insights in this chapter, which largely started with Wayne and which have continued to develop with the help of other gurus in and out of the financial world, work for you as well as they have for me and all those who are important to me both personally and professionally.

My wife, Jill, and me with Dr. Wayne W. Dyer, 2001.

DEFINING TRUE WEALTH

Perhaps the most important lesson I've incorporated into my life has been how to define my true wealth. Before making the conscious decision to settle down, raise a family, purchase a home, and start my financial firm, my previous business had empowered me to create a lifestyle for myself that enabled me to spend a month in each of 65 different countries around the world. This concept was introduced to me in Roger Dawson's tape series titled Making Your Life an Adventure. Most of my sojourns took my one-man tent and me to developing countries throughout South and Central America, Southeast Asia, and Africa.

Teaching school children about money in Sipi Falls, Uganda, 1995.

This was a time to learn about diverse cultures and political viewpoints, as well as about new ways to grow a profitable business with a focus on people and our environment. In the process, I also learned about my relationship to money and certainly about myself.

At first, I considered the gracious people and gregarious children in small villages such as on Taveuni, Fiji; Bukit Lawang, Sumatra; and Sipi Falls, Uganda, to be poor. After all, they lived in diminutive houses with dirt floors and no windows. Families didn't have cars, televisions, iPods, or IRAs, but I quickly realized that most of the villagers were undeniably happy. While most Americans mistakenly observed these villagers' lives as grueling and arduous, the villagers always seemed to smile a great deal, enjoy each other's company, and work together in harmony. Although these fun and easygoing locals owned very few of the creature comforts that Americans have become accustomed to, were they actually poor?

Helping to prepare dinner in Taveuni, Fiji, 1991.

Can you imagine if I shared stories of the markets in my home country piled with food flown in from around the world, stories of doctors who gave out pills to stop people from eating, and stories of cars so abundant that they clogged the roads and slowed the traffic to the pace of a bicycle? They would never have believed me. And if they finally did, they might have considered us rich, but would they truly have considered us wealthy?

I pondered then, and continue to wonder, whether American problems stem from having too much, rather than too little. And because of these problems, we have what most call stress, a concept the villagers I lived with had never heard of. Being rich and being wealthy seem to be synonymous. However, I would argue that there's a big difference between the two. We all know people who have accumulated significant money in their lives but who just aren't joyful. They may have numerous failed relationships and children who don't talk to them. I would consider these people to be rich but certainly not wealthy, as I feel that true wealth comes from a grounded place in the heart. You also may know people who face financial challenges but are genuinely happy, with many close friends and a passion for life. These people have wealth in their lives even though they have not accumulated riches. This lesson would quickly be reinforced once back in the States.

Shortly after returning home following a life-changing, six-month stint in East Africa, I visited a chic restaurant and witnessed an aggravated woman send back her ahi tuna steak because it had been cooked medium instead of medium-rare. Later I watched a man struggle over whether to order a fruit plate for dessert and stick to his diet or splurge on an ice-cream sundae dripping with caramel and piled with pecans.

Does any of this sound familiar? I, too, am often faced with such dilemmas. But then I think about the villagers' lives. Imagine eating cassava, also known as manioc or yuca, at every meal. Do you know what cassava is? You will be hard-pressed to see it in American grocery stores, but it is a staple throughout developing countries around the globe. On the outside, it looks a little like a woody shrub; it tastes like a tough, extra-starchy potato. Cassava is extensively cultivated as an annual crop in tropical regions because its edible root provides a major source of carbohydrates. The folks in the villages had learned to cook it creatively. They boiled it, fried it, beat it to a pulp and dipped it in sauce. But every day it was still cassava. Over time I grew so accustomed to it that I ceased to taste it at all. Although I am glad my diet doesn't consist of cassava, I'm very aware that I don't need the abundance of food that presents itself in the United States. And that has impacted not only my day-to-day choices and my financial future, but also my sense of well-being.

CAN LESS BE MORE?

Some of my clients who are saving for their retirement dreams have shared with me that although they are working harder than ever before and have successfully increased their standard of living, they are feeling less fulfilled. Many are diligently striving to acquire things and build wealth for their family. This is a dignified ambition and my job is to help guide them so they can eventually live the life they have always imagined. Many of us share similar goals, but

I think it is important to ask ourselves whether this path of accumulating possessions is truly leading to a life of abundance and contentment.

I will be the first to admit that it is satisfying to have some of the niceties of life. However, I also find myself pondering whether having more is better. Does it truly bring greater happiness into our lives? I observe people who must work harder and harder to support their acquisitions, which generates a great deal of stress in their lives. If we set a goal to acquire possessions, it is important that we build a gap between the costs of servicing these acquisitions and the income we are earning.

I recently read a story called "Life Is Like a Cup of Coffee." This narrative has a powerful message that I want to share with you:

> A group of alumni, highly established in their careers, got together to visit their old university professor. Conversation soon turned into complaints about stress in work and life. Offering his guests coffee, the professor went to the kitchen and returned with a large pot of coffee and an assortment of cups— porcelain, plastic, glass, crystal, some plain looking, some expensive, some exquisite—telling his guests to help themselves.

> When all the students had a cup of coffee in hand, the professor said: "If you noticed, all the nice looking expensive cups have been taken up, leaving behind the plain and cheap ones. While it is normal for you to want only the best for yourselves, that is the source of your problems and stress.

"Be assured that the cup itself adds no quality to the coffee. In most cases it is just more expensive and in some cases even hides what we drink. What all of you really wanted was coffee, not the cup, but you consciously went for the best cups...And then you began eyeing each other's cups. Now consider this: Life is the coffee; the jobs, money, and position in society are the cups. They are just tools to hold and contain life, and the type of cup we have does not define or change the quality of life we live. Sometimes, by concentrating only on the cup, we fail to enjoy the coffee. Savor the coffee, not the cups! The happiest people don't have the best of everything. They just make the best of everything. Live simply. Love generously. Care deeply. Speak kindly."

Warren Buffett, widely regarded as one of the wealthiest and most successful investors in the world, says much the same thing. "The happiest people do not necessarily have the best things," he asserts. "They simply appreciate the things they have." Buffett still lives in the same three-bedroom house in mid-town Omaha that he bought after getting married 50 years ago. He says that he has everything he needs in that house, which is not walled or fenced in. He preaches that we shouldn't buy more than what we really need. He drives his own car everywhere he goes, having forgone a driver and security people. And although he owns the world's largest private jet company, he always flies commercial airlines.

Like Buffett, I believe that one of the keys to life is living below your means in order to have the time to be happy. Another is finding a way to reduce your stress and increase your joy. So when my meal arrives a little overcooked or I have to choose between ice cream and fruit, I give thanks for the life I have. When was the last time you took a moment out of your busy schedule to give thanks for all that you have? Gratitude is the direct gateway to happiness and the indirect route to financial plenty, since it helps us to celebrate what we have rather than focusing on what we don't.

AN ATTITUDE OF GRATITUDE

Wayne Dyer often talks about the importance of being grateful for what we already have in our lives. By focusing on what we're grateful for, more of that very thing comes into our lives. Why? As I've mentioned previously, what we think about expands. This applies just as much to money as anything else.

To help me remember to be grateful, I carry a gratitude stone with me most of the time. I also offer gratitude stones to all my clients and to audiences who attend my speaking engagements. What is a gratitude stone, you ask? It is a small stone that you carry with you in your pocket or purse or leave on your desk at work. The idea is to put it in a place where you are likely to come in contact with it throughout your day. Each time you see or touch the stone, it will act as a small reminder to you to be grateful. I find this to be most beneficial during challenging times. Think of it as your tool to attract good thoughts.

In the morning as I get ready to leave for work, my thoughts are often already on my activities for the day. I put on my watch, grab my smart phone, wallet, car keys, and lastly my black onyx gratitude stone. It is my reminder to stop for just a brief moment and ask myself, "What am I thankful for at this moment?" It is amazing how that slows me down, grounds me and shifts my outlook. Each time I see or touch this ancient rock throughout the day, I'm reminded to be grateful for what I have today and for what will come tomorrow.

As I've mentioned before, I am a true believer that what we think about expands. That's why it's so important to be appreciative of what we have achieved. That's fairly easy during the good times. Showing gratitude, however, is even more important when facing extreme hardships.

SHIFTING FINANCIAL PRIORITIES

In March 2011, earthquakes, a tsunami, and a nuclear disaster took a toll on the people of Japan as well as on their already beleaguered financial markets. Clearly, the largest recorded earthquake in that nation's history has brought daunting new challenges to the social and economic fabric of Japan. Just weeks earlier, my wife's homeland of New Zealand had been rocked by the worst earthquake in its history, which leveled most of beautiful downtown Christchurch. In October 2012, the United States experienced tragedy as Hurricane Sandy, the largest Atlantic hurricane on record, hammered the Northeast's coastal towns. A year later, a two-mile wide tornado flattened Moore, an Oklahoma City suburb.

Life's priorities take on a starkly different cast after such devastating tragedies. "I realize how much I have wasted," Ms. Kusaka, a Japanese citizen stated to a New York Times reporter as she hurried with her boyfriend through empty streets in the normally glittering Ginza shopping district where two weeks after the earthquake streetlamps were still darkened to save electricity. "This whole incident has changed people's outlooks," she added. Indeed, analysts affirm that the triple disaster has jolted the Japanese into a new reality, sapping the materialistic, feel-good-at-any-cost spirit and replacing it with a focus on helping others and a back-to-basics mood.

No place on earth is safe from natural disasters or economic cycles. They are inevitable. We know they will happen and we know that planning and accumulated knowledge can help minimize the totality of damage. That approach works with investing. Shifting one's financial priorities is essential in today's new world economy. Let's face it: The real measure of wealth is our peace of mind, family, friends and the legacy we leave to others. This applies to companies as much as individuals, since they too leave a legacy.

SPIRITUAL CAPITALISM

It is both sad and unfortunate to read in the news how often a company or CEO gets indicted for improper or unethical conduct. Examples include companies that knowingly import toys with lead paint, CEOs who embezzle money from their company or falsify business records, or oil companies that don't take responsibility for environmental catastrophes they've caused. The question of ethics has become a heightened one as we witness the scandalous behavior of so many companies in recent years. Maybe these companies should start focusing on a concept I have been reading about lately called Spiritual Capitalism.

Ode Magazine writes:

> Spiritual Capitalism doesn't mean prayer sessions on the factory floor and guided meditations in the boardroom. At least it doesn't have to. What it does mean is the success of an enterprise is measured by values like 'integrity' and 'commitment' as much as by targets like 'efficiency' and 'profitability. Whether you're the CEO of a major multinational company or the head of your own small firm, you are in the service industry, and the services rendered must benefit not just yourself and your shareholders, but the planet and other people as well.

Spiritual capitalism enriches our quality of life, creates a healthier and more engaged populace, and ultimately creates new markets. "Many companies today overlook the tremendous value added to their bottom line when they are not willing or able to do what is necessary to structure and maintain what might be termed best-practice work cultures," Jim Lee told me. Lee is a former executive director of Abilitree, a non-profit organization in Bend, Oregon, that helps empower those with disabilities to grow their independence. The focus for anyone looking to incorporate spirituality in business needs to be on more than just financial success. The focus should be on doing the right thing for your customers and clients as well as for your community.

Spiritual capitalism should also be a consideration in how we work with our employees. Many employees have unfortunately experienced employers with the mindset that their employees are fortunate to have any employment during difficult economic times. These employers offer what many consider to be very low wages with little to no benefits. Even though we have been walking in the shadow of a serious recession, other employers believe that embracing values like compassion and sincere care for employees is a smart business move, since a happier employee is a more productive employee.

I believe that any employer who contributes to the prosperity of his or her staff and the world around them will prosper in turn. Take Ben Cohen and Jerry Greenfield, two successful capitalists who measure their success by more than just corporate profits. Ben & Jerry's, their famous ice cream company from Vermont, was founded on—and remains dedicated to—a sustainable corporate concept of linked prosperity with a focus on its employees, the community, and its consumers. The company's mission consists of three interrelated parts: product mission, economic mission, and social mission. Central to Ben & Jerry's over-arching mission is the belief that all three parts must thrive equally in a manner that commands deep respect for individuals in and outside the company and supports the communities of which they are a part. The company's social mission focuses on operating the organization in a way that actively recognizes the central role business plays in society. They do this by initiating innovative ways to improve the quality of life locally, nationally, and internationally. Ben & Jerry's foundation gives millions of dollars annually to charitable causes that support the founding values of the company.

The Calvert Group is another company demonstrating that a company's spiritual culture not only makes a very positive impact on our world, it spawns a competitive advantage. In 1982, the company created socially responsible mutual funds that exclude tobacco, alcohol, firearms, and other harmful products from their investment portfolios. Today, Calvert has expanded its focus. In addition to eliminating companies that are injurious, it searches for companies that go out of their way to do good. Over the years, more and more of my clients have asked for socially responsible investments.

This has certainly been an area where money and spirit meet. The late Earl Nightingale, author of *The Strangest Secret,* stated: "We are at our very best, and we are happiest, when we are fully engaged in work we enjoy on the journey toward the goal we've established for ourselves. It gives meaning to our time off and comfort to our sleep. It makes everything else in life so wonderful, so worthwhile." By focusing on doing the right things for others and our community, we can all flourish and keep spiritual capitalism alive. This will benefit everyone in the long run, whether climbing a mountain or pursuing your quest toward financial self- actualization.

"How You Climb a Mountain Is More Important Than Reaching the Top"

My mom, my dad, and Yvon Chouinard—the founder and owner of Patagonia, the world-renowned outdoor clothing and equipment company—have always seen eye to eye. My parents taught me early in life to do things right. I was fortunate to grow up in beautiful Upstate New York. Many people seem to think that Upstate means the northern portion of Manhattan when in reality Upstate New York is an outdoor lover's paradise located a few hours north of New York City. Its Adirondack State Park is the largest state park in the country with six million acres of spectacular wilderness, over 4,000 bodies of water, and more ski areas than any other region of the country. It was home to the 1932 and 1980 Winter Olympics in majestic Lake Placid. It was also the place where I learned to rock climb on the granite walls of the Adirondacks.

Although I have always had a fear of heights, over the years, as my technique has improved, I have learned to trust my equipment, climbing partners, and myself as long as I don't focus on the drop below me. While the exhilarating feeling of accomplishment when I reach the top of a climb keeps me coming back for more, the camaraderie is what I most enjoy. John Krog, my climbing mentor and early rock-climbing guide at Smith Rock, Oregon, would preach that the biggest muscle one needs in rock climbing is the one between your ears. I could not agree more as you must stay focused, not give up, and forge ahead even when you may feel there is no way to get past the most challenging section known as the crux.

Speaking of cruxes, my ultimate rock climbing adventure happened in Yosemite National Park during the spring of 2009 with John and two other climbing partners, Matt Gadow and Jim Gross. In all my travels around the world I have never been to a more majestic place. Yosemite is one of the world's greatest big-wall climbing areas. Although our group had considerable experience climbing multi-pitch routes, unlike so many who travel from all over the world to attempt the multi-day accents we were not world-class climbers. Even so, our goal was to climb Sunnyside Bench to the right side of Yosemite Falls. That certainly got my attention, as I have never been 700 feet off the deck!

In Yosemite, 2009.

Another hub I spent time learning to climb was the Shawangunk
Ridge, also known as The Gunks. This rock-climbing mecca of
the East is located in the Catskill Mountains of New York State.
This is where Chouinard was the first to free climb the first pitch
of Matinee in the early 1960s. Free climbing is where the climber uses only hands, feet and other parts of the body to ascend.
No ropes are involved. At the time, his route was considered the
toughest climb at The Gunks even for those using ropes.

Today, Chouinard's photo hangs prominently in my office conference room not simply because he was a rock-climbing pioneer with many first ascents, but because no one embodies *spiritual capitalism* more for me than this legendary rock climber, environmentalist, and businessman. Patagonia is one of the most respected and environmentally responsible companies anywhere because of its leader.

Chouinard has always epitomized social and environmental responsibility. In the early 1970s when Chouinard became aware that the steel pitons he had developed were causing significant damage to the rocks he and his partners regularly climbed, he revolutionized the sport by introducing aluminum gear that would not cause destruction to rock faces. Imagine what our world would look like if more businessmen followed his conscientious lead.

In one of my favorite books, *Let My People Go Surfing: The Education of a Reluctant Businessman,* Chouinard shares his stories of first ascents including the North American Wall on Yosemite's El Capitan. This colossal section in the middle part of this 3,000-foot granite monolith resembles the shape of our continent. The route was considered the most technically challenging in all of the Yosemite Valley and possibly the world. Previously considered impossible to climb, Chouinard scaled this wall in 1964 using no fixed ropes! After experiencing the Yosemite Fall climb, I have the utmost respect for Chouinard and his contemporaries who pioneered big-wall climbing in Yosemite.

Chouinard's book is more than just a series of epic escapades. It is the story of a man who focused on doing the right thing for his employees, his customers, and the environment. Chouinard was one of the first to set standards with employee-friendly guidelines. In 1984, Patagonia began offering its employees on-site child care. A company cafeteria was opened providing "healthy, mostly vegetarian food" and his employees were compensated for volunteering on local projects that benefitted the environment. At the time, this was unheard of in corporate America. However, Chouinard's principles would prove profitable not only for himself, but for many of those he dealt with. When an environmental assessment of Patagonia in the early 90s revealed the unforeseen result that cotton had turned into an ominously harmful product for the environment, Chouinard committed Patagonia to using all pesticide-free cotton. This new demand created the organic cotton industry in California.

Patagonia annually contributes the greater of 1 percent of sales or 10 percent of profits to different environmental causes. The approach has led this new style of responsible business to annual revenue of $230 million. According to *Fortune magazine,* Chouinard is possibly the most successful outdoor industry businessman alive today. Meanwhile, Chouinard identifies himself as more of "a climber, a surfer, a kayaker, a skier, and a blacksmith" than a CEO.

How many leading entrepreneurs would say, "The Lee Iacoccas, Donald Trumps, and Jack Welches of the business world are heroes to no one except other businessmen with similar values"? It is interesting how, years ago, I devoured Iacocca's *An Autobiography,* Trump's *Art of the Deal,* and Welch's *The GE Way.* At the time these three business leaders were champions in my mind. Although I admire what each has been able to accomplish in their business careers, today I have far greater respect for men like Yvon Chouinard and Ben Cohen and Jerry Greenfield than I do Wall Street titans who all too often focus more on share price and executive bonuses than on people.

Chouinard, Cohen, and Greenfield embody a soulfulness that is often missing in today's business world. They are connected to family, friends, employees, and customers as well as to the environment. And they've profited as a result. Many of us, however, can be connected in other ways that are not so helpful.

WE ARE SO CONNECTED THAT WE ARE DISCONNECTED

Are we teaching our children by example to be disconnected from their environment? A few years ago I had an opportunity to be a chaperone for my daughter's class trip to Crater Lake National Park. This is a place of immeasurable beauty that doubles as an outstanding outdoor laboratory and classroom. The majestic, deep blue lake fills a 2,000-foot volcanic caldera with sheer surrounding cliffs and two picturesque islands. The moment we entered the bus for the two-hour ride to the park, I noticed that almost every child had tuned into his or her iPod, Game Boy or DS video game. Many of the young children even had their own cell phones. There was no conversing with each other. Their focus was not on telling stories or playing games together but on using these electronic devices to withdraw from one another and the events of the day. I felt an overwhelming sadness as I questioned whether many children of today are missing out on their childhoods. I asked myself, *Are seven year olds going on seventeen already?*

How will this affect their future? Will they ever learn the essential skills of communication? What will this mean for our future society?

I embrace technology and how it benefits us in countless ways, but I began to ponder its potential side effects. The original purpose of technology was to increase productivity so that we could have more time. Today we are moving through life faster than ever before, but do we really have more time? Are our children by-products of our appetite for speed? Tom Monaghan, the founder of Dominos, began his pizza empire by guaranteeing delivery in 30 minutes or less or the pie was free. He states that his company is in the delivery business and not the pizza business. I certainly agree with him; most of us have not ordered Dominos because it is gourmet but because it fulfills our need for speed. Are we feeding our fast-paced existence to where it is only satisfied when it gets more adrenaline flowing? What are our children learning from us?

This reminds me of the story of a son and his dad. The dad always brought his briefcase home from the office and this confused the son. The son said: "Dad, why is it that when you come home from work you always bring your brief-case?" The father replied that it was because he could not get all of his work done at the office. The little boy said: "Dad, can't they put you in a slower group?"

The truth is that some of us probably need to be put into a slower group. And we certainly need to move into a slower group and decompress on vacation.

LIFE LESSONS FROM THE BIG ISLAND

My wife Jill and I recently visited the Big Island of Hawaii as we had heard that it was the most tranquil of this Pacific Island chain and best maintained the "aloha spirit," which is the charm, warmth, and sincerity that Hawaii's people are known for.

Aside from a flight over the active Kilauea volcano, better known to the Hawaiians as Pele, the Goddess of Fire, there were no tourist attractions we needed to check off a list. No luaus or hula dancers for us. Instead, it was all about getting away, enjoying nature and each other's company.

I am a planner. It is what I do for a living. But the only thing I planned for this tropical retreat was to be disengaged from the work I love. This was to be a vacation by design rather than by default. It would be a time to slow down. I knew it would take a couple of days to ease into the pace of island life, but I was full of pride as I set my e-mail on auto response. I would not be online all week.

I was determinedly disconnected, but this was not the case with many of the visitors to this serene island. Each morning we awoke to the rising sun and the sounds of the sea. While relishing the ocean views from our lanai, we noticed a young father pushing a baby cart on the pathway below with one hand while responding to e-mails on his smart phone with the other. I felt sad as I recognized that he was not experiencing the important things right in front of him. Did he even see the Honu (Hawaiian Green Turtles) sleeping on the sand? What about the vibrant Apapane flying from palm tree to palm tree? He was not connecting to nature and most importantly he was not connecting to his child.

After the sun had risen, the aroma of 100 percent Kona coffee led us to the resort's open-air coffee shop. I immediately understood why this delectable morning delight comes at such a premium. We sat on the couch overlooking a tranquil pond of Koi. Most of the café's patrons had a laptop or tablet in hand. E-mails were being answered. Some people were reading the *Wall Street Journal* or their home newspaper online. Others were posting photos on Facebook. Although their intent may have been to leave their fast-paced lifestyle at home, they were continuing to be connected, which actually disconnected them from their present surroundings.

Jack Johnson, the Hawaiian singer-songwriter, sings about his fear of a tech-addicted future in his latest acoustic number "Ones and Zeros." In a recent *Rolling Stone* interview he states: "I see girls on the beach that never let go of their phones. It's kind of crazy. We're all accepting this idea that kids are constantly moving their fingers around these little flat screens. Is it worth it? Do we let books just slide away?"

It's not easy for most of us to disconnect. As I witnessed on the school bus, it is easy to spot how our children pick up on our habits. But we can choose to slow down and smell the air and the dirt as well as the flowers. By making a conscious decision to disconnect, I began to feel liberated and in flow with life like the molten lava we had viewed flowing into the sea just days earlier. This is what the Aloha spirit is all about.

THE ALOHA SPIRIT

The Aloha Spirit of Hawaii is the harmonization of mind and heart within each person. It refers to a powerful way to resolve any problem, accomplish any goal, and to achieve any state of mind or body that you desire. By being overly connected to the world, we can actually become disconnected to the things that matter in our lives. I hope you'll take action to reduce your information intake. Do it and you'll find yourself with much greater peace of mind and time to spare. You'll have internalized a bit of the Aloha Spirit that guides the lives of so many Hawaiians.

I have always found it intriguing that hundreds of Hawaiians have moved to Central Oregon over the years. Could it be our volcanic landscape that reminds them of the islands? Could it be the attitude of friendly acceptance for which Central Oregon and the Hawaiian Islands are both known? Bill Keale is one of Central Oregon's most celebrated and beloved musicians, recognized for his beautiful voice and Slack Key Guitar skills. He is a native Hawaiian who comes from a long lineage of legendary musicians such as his Uncle Moe Keale and cherished cousin Israel Kamakawiwoʻole, better recognized as Bruddah IZ. IZ's voice became famous outside Hawaii with his medley of *Over the Rainbow* and *What a Wonderful World*. Bill sings a version of IZ's heartwarming yet sad song titled *Hawaii 1978*, which profoundly shares how he believes King Kamehameha and his wife would feel if they were still alive today and saw the Islands in their present state.

Contemporary Hawaii is a far cry from its past. Development remains a huge issue and land prices are out of reach for much of the native population. The Islands' limited natural resources are being seriously tapped. The reflective lyrics sum up the problem:

How would they feel about the changes of our land? Could you just imagine if they were around and saw highways on their sacred grounds? How would they feel about modern city life? Tears would come from each others' eyes as they would stop to realize that our people are in great danger now.

Too many of us suffer from that same threat of over-development that's sucking the life out of us. No amount of money can help when that happens.

Gerry Lopez is another prominent Hawaiian to call Bend, Oregon, home. He is a legendary surfing icon who led the short-board revolution surfing craze of the early 1970s. He won the Pipeline Masters of Oahu's North Shore competition in 1972 and 1973, which has since been named the Gerry Lopez Pipeline Masters. I was given his autobiography of entertaining stories, *Surf Is Where You Find It,* to read on my Hawaiian vacation. His writings resonated with me and my growing concerns for our society: "Surfing happens best when it's the present; the past is behind and the future not yet. The only thing of interest is what's here and now." This is a timeless message from an icon for the soul of surfing. Today Gerry owns a successful surf and paddleboard company. With his Aloha spirit and focus on spiritual capitalism, he has been as successful with his company as he was in his earlier surfing career.

Working hard and having a strong work ethic is very important, but I find that one of the best ways to grow a strong business—or one's assets—is to do so while still keeping a reasonable pace in one's life. I hear people say that someday their life will settle down. I do not believe this will automatically happen. Settling life down is a choice. Do you remember Wayne Dyer's message? *Remember yesterday, dream about tomorrow but live today.* Those words can serve you—and your finances—well as long as you can get out of your own way.

Chapter 12

OVERCOMING THE BIGGEST OBSTACLE—
YOU!

The secret of success is constancy to purpose.

—Benjamin Disraeli

A re you the weak link when it comes to your pre- and post-retirement financial success? Benjamin Graham, a prominent economist and investor known for coaching Warren Buffett, had the following to say in his book *The Intelligent Investor* when observing the irrationality that seized the market in the Great Depression: "The investor's chief problem—and even his worst enemy—is likely to be himself." Graham recognized that investing requires a certain mentality. "Individuals who cannot master their emotions," he said, "are ill-suited to profit from the investment process."

To illustrate that point, consider stand-up paddling (SUP), an ancient sport of Hawaiian heritage that was reintroduced to the modern water sports world by surfing icons Laird Hamilton and David Kalama. Today it is an emerging global sport that has experienced an enormous rise in popularity. Surfing legend Gerry Lopez has helped to make it ubiquitous in my hometown of Bend, Oregon. I believe one of the reasons for its popularity is that unlike surfing, paddleboarding is very easy to learn. It also offers great fun as well as a serious workout, so if you haven't experienced it yet, give it a try. I have had the good fortune of learning proper technique over the past few years from my friend and former big wave surfer Alistair Paterson. As we were paddling early one morning before work, I could not help but correlate the similarities between navigating the Deschutes River and navigating the stock market.

Stand up paddleboarding on the Deschutes River in Bend, Oregon, 2012.

As a long-term observer of the markets, it never ceases to amaze me how violent and rapid market moves can be in both directions. Since 1946, there have been ten bear markets where the market decline has exceeded 20 percent. The average decline has been 35 percent.

One of the best ways to describe this volatility of U.S. equity markets is to compare it to the rapids Alistair and I encountered as we approached Benham Falls, the largest falls on the Deschutes River. We had started off on placid waters, but quickly had to paddle with increasing intensity to power our way upriver against the current. That's when I discovered that while you think you can prepare for rapids, you don't really know when they're going to show up or how strong they'll be. Sometimes you hear different noises from the river, but it ends up being nothing. Sometimes you hear very little, and all of a sudden you are in a tumultuous portion of the river. While you are always on the lookout and think you are prepared, it is virtually impossible to be fully primed; and yet there is no way to avoid the rapids if you want to reach your destination. You can anticipate the rapids and prepare as well as possible, but when they come, you are still anxious. The one thing you cannot do is bail off of the paddleboard as this would guarantee you not reaching your destination. Failure is not an option.

Preparing for the rapids during the second half of your financial journey is about designing an effective retirement and distribution plan. Creating your financial hierarchy of needs, asset, and strategy allocation will help get you to your investment destination. Even so, the journey will not always be totally smooth. Rapids will be encountered and you will need to triumph.

When you observe the many economic challenges our country currently faces, I suggest asking yourself, *haven't we had some of these situations in one form or another for the past 50 years?* Do you remember sitting in gas lines in 1973 during the oil embargo? Do you remember when inflation rose above 13 percent in 1980? Do you remember Black Monday in October 1987 when the U.S. stock market dropped 20 percent in one day? What about the dot-com crash shortly after 9/11? Then there was 2008, the worst year in stock market history. These and many other financial rapids have been encountered on an irregular basis for half a century; I suspect we will continue to encounter rapids as we paddle down the river of our lifetime. As we've discussed, the worst move in the middle of rapids is to bail off the paddleboard. All too often, however, that's exactly what investors do.

Much like changing your putting stroke right before the biggest putt of your life, individuals often abandon process and technique in the very moments when those are most important. Okay, I know I'm mixing my metaphors here, but the point remains the same. Relying on proven investment processes, as described in previous chapters, can help ensure that you safely navigate your way to your final destination.

Alistair and I exerted much effort to reach Benham Falls, and then carefully turned our paddleboards around in the direction of the current. Our hard work and persistence of staying the course paid off. The rest of the journey was relaxed as we paddled effortlessly with the river, enjoying the Central Oregon scenery and making slight adjustments as needed along the way. Had our attitudes been different, we might have quit before reaching our goal or tensed up to the point where we could barely paddle. Instead, we went with the flow mentally even as we fought against the current physically. You could do a lot worse than adopting a similarly tenacious-meets-go-with-the-flow approach to investing.

GRAZE ON GOOD GRASS

Where do we go from here? I wish I had all of the answers and could confidently tell you where our economy or the markets will be in the future. Every financial expert seems to have his or her own opinion or timeline. Although I will not prognosticate, I will share some insights with the intention of bringing greater clarity as well as reducing some of the fear that unfortunately has spread throughout the United States and abroad.

The investment climate in the U.S. is often exacerbated by our 24/7 financial commentators whose primary objective seems to be increasing their Nielsen ratings. As we feed our minds with a barrage of negative news, we only exacerbate the pessimistic and destructive sentiment that currently prevails. We need to be cautious about the information we allow to dominate our daily thoughts. Fear and pessimism sell and the media knows it. I consider many of the financial networks that highlight headlines containing words like *panic* and *collapse* to be financial pornography. Former General Electric CEO Jack Welch compares many financial journalists to weather forecasters in a hurricane who become giddy as they describe the biggest storm of their careers. Their excitement is understandable, but some perspective gets lost in the fray.

Because I believe that what we think about expands, for years I contemplated the idea of killing our family TV. Fearful of being disconnected from the world, however, my wife Jill and I always kept up on current events and thought it was our duty to know everything happening around the globe as well in our community. We found ourselves going to sleep to the hostility of the 11 o'clock news. During the night our subconscious minds would ponder the last messages they had been fed. In the morning we would immediately flick on the news and start our days with this same negativity and gloom. Was this benefiting us? Five years ago we finally pulled the plug on our TV. We said no more to fear. It is amazing how our world shifted as we started focusing even more on the things that truly matter: our family, friends, and community.

Invest in Yourself Instead of in Fear

Winston Churchill said: "Let our advance worrying become advance thinking and planning." Planning and preparation make the difference in the success of many things. To paraphrase Franklin Delano Roosevelt, who led us out of the Great Depression, I believe the main thing to be fearful about today is fear itself. Thoughts of doubt and fear never accomplish anything and never can. Thoughts fly from your mind to connect with whatever you are thinking about. James Allen in his classic essay "As a Man Thinketh" writes: "A man cannot directly choose his circumstances but he can choose his thoughts, and so indirectly, yet surely shape his circumstances." We must focus on squashing the fear that is often prevalent in our minds. Trusting ourselves in the midst of a world seemingly gone mad is a wise use of our intentions.

So what are your intentions moving forward regarding your years of financial independence?

What are you aiming for in your life and your financial future?

I'm reminded of Wayne Gretzky's summation regarding how he plays hockey: "I skate to where the puck is going to be, not to where it has been." Unfortunately when it comes to investing, fearful thoughts based on past downturns seem to preoccupy the minds of many. That makes it very difficult for them to keep a positive outlook. Now more than ever we need to change what we focus on. What we focus on expands. I know, I'm starting to repeat myself. But I also know that when I focus on fear, I experience more fear and I find more reasons to be fearful. This can become a self-fulfilling prophecy that leads to a damaging downward spiral. Over the years I have made a conscious effort not to worry about the things in my life that I have absolutely no control over. I have no control over the weather—or the stock and real estate markets—but I can control how I observe all of them. I can even control how I perceive their impact on me. And I can plan in a way that mitigates that impact.

These days, instead of asking, *Why me?* I ask myself whether there could be a gift in whatever perceived adversity I'm experiencing. How could that single shift impact you? Imagine that instead of spending time listening to the news or reading the newspaper to find out why you should be fearful, you used that time and energy to do something more meaningful and beneficial. Read something uplifting, listen to something empowering, learn a new skill, connect with others or enjoy your time in nature. For over 20 years, I have used my time in my car to listen to CDs on motivation, sales techniques, philosophy and, of course, investing. If you were to listen to an educational CD or podcast on your way to and from work for just 30 minutes a day, that would total 125 hours each year. This equates to not just one but several college courses. Maybe that's why Zig Ziglar referred to his car as Automobile University. Just think about what you could learn about personal finance during this time.

AN ILLUSION OF LINEARITY

One of the lessons you would learn is that linearity is pure illusion where investing is concerned. Let's take, well, you as an example. When you were basking in times of economic glory as your home was increasing in value on a daily basis and your 401(k) continued to reach new highs, you probably expected this favorable trend to continue on into the future without letting up. Most people did. Following a similar pattern during the Great Recession, people focusing on their current challenges felt that these distressing times were here for good and that we would experience a permanent downtrend. Much of our society seems to buy into this way of thinking, but the world does not work in a linear fashion. History has shown us that the only constant in life is change. Market downturns are a natural part of our free market system. They have occurred throughout history and will continue to do so. In fact, since 1929 there have been 15 bear markets. They all eventually end. At some point, downturns may even be recognized as part of a cycle that actually includes years of slow and steady upward progress.

A Bear Market Is the Temporary Eruption of a Permanent Uptrend

The word recession has become taboo in current times. Most people do not realize what you know—that our economy averages a recession about every nine years. This has and always will be a reality to our economy. When we take this historical perspective and realize that there has never been a down real estate or stock market that has not bounced back to hit an all-time high, it becomes that much easier to deal with challenging times.

Staying calm amid market turmoil is not easy. Fears of further decline can make investors feel skittish. This is absolutely the wrong time for investors to panic and throw in the towel. The cost of missing a market rebound is significant. Remember the couple that had been referred to my practice? The man gloated about the fact that he had liquidated his entire retirement portfolio just before the markets crashed in 2008. I congratulated him and asked him when he had reinvested his retirement funds back into the market as the Dow Jones Industrial Average (DIJA) had climbed more than 125 percent from its low on March 6, 2009. In a dejected tone he stated that the markets had been just too high to invest in and that he was waiting for them to retreat before reinvesting. Had he remained invested, his assets would likely have grown by 25 percent—a profit he missed out on. I had to explain that by attempting to time the market, he would have to be lucky not just once, but twice. The odds of accomplishing such a feat are not favorable.

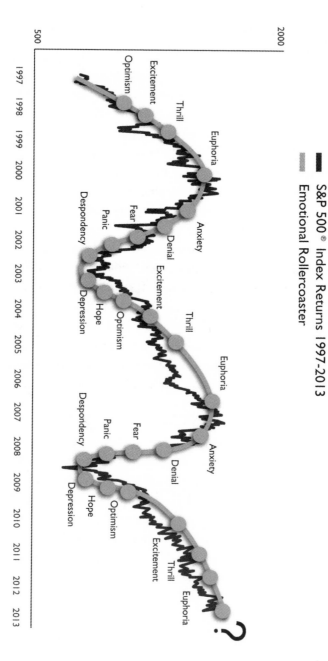

S&P 500 ® Index Returns 1997-2013
Emotional Rollercoaster

As you can see from this 17-year look at the S&P 500, stock market volatility and investor emotional reactions move with absolute synchronicity.

Historically when coming out of a bear market, the best equity market performance is generated in the first three months following the bottom. As it is practically impossible to predict the bottom in a market, investors need to remain invested. If not, like the gentleman in my office experienced, they risk missing out on the period of highest performance and jeopardize attractive long-term performance. Investing icon Peter Lynch of Fidelity Investments said: *Which way the next 1,000 to 2,000 points in the market will go is anybody's guess, but I believe strongly that the next 10,000, 20,000 and 40,000 points will be up.* The markets have been undulating like a yo-yo but Lynch was on to something as the U.S. stock markets recently hit new heights just four years after the recent lows.

THE YO-YO EFFECT

It is all too common to focus on our current dilemmas and challenges without learning from history. But sometimes we need help putting the past in perspective, especially where finances are concerned. To help you with that, I want you to visualize a cute boy with his baseball cap sitting backward on his head as he starts walking up a sinuous mountain road with a yoyo in hand. The undulating yoyo symbolizes the economy, real estate or stock market. As the yoyo goes up everyone is elated. As it falls everyone feels scared and depressed. As the yoyo starts its next ascent we all celebrate with exuberance. Then before we know it, gravity takes over and the yoyo faces a downward spiral. Suddenly our stomachs begin to feel queasy with apprehension. It is up to each of us to choose whether we focus on the rising and falling yoyo or the boy. You see, they both reach the top of the mountain with its majestic views at the exact same time.

So let's take that analogy and apply it to relatively recent history. October 19, 1987, is an ominous date known as Black Monday. The Black Monday decline was the largest one-day percentage decline in stock market history. The Dow Jones Industrial Average dropped by 508 points to 1739 (22.6 percent). By the end of October, stock markets in Hong Kong had fallen 45.8 percent, Australia 41.8 percent and the United Kingdom 26.4 percent. New Zealand's market was hit especially hard, falling about 60 percent. Investors around the world thought the end was near and fear overtook the financial world. Interestingly, the DJIA was not only positive for the 1987 calendar year but would close on December 31st, 1987, at an all-time record high of 1,939 points.

Just 25 years later, the DJIA can now fluctuate in a single trading day by as much as Black Monday's record-breaking 508 points. If someone had told you back then that in 2013 the DJIA would surpass 15,000, you would have thought they had lost their senses. The economy may continue its yo-yo-like movement with ups and downs. It's up to us to remember to keep our perspective by learning from the past and rising to the challenge of the future.

AN ECONOMIC CRISIS IS A TERRIBLE THING TO WASTE

While the past recession has been a very emotional time period for investors, it has been exponentially worse for those at or near retirement. Over-investing in our emotions, however, is bad news for our financial investments. Chuck Widger, the executive chairman of Brinker Capital, sums up my points eloquently:

To reap the rewards of prudent investing, you'll have to fol-low the time-tested approach of staying invested for the long term—even though it's usually accompanied by a time-tested case of anxiety. The flow of individual investors' money shows that in the battle between emotions and sound strategy, emotion has taken the upper hand. Many investors abandon long-term strategies for the perceived safety of cash. It's hu-man nature: In challenging times, our emotions tell us to pull out of the markets and run for the hills. However, this creates two big problems. First, it's hard to see opportunities from far up in the hills. And second, when markets turn around, it can take too long to climb back down and get invested again. Selling during periods of market stress may cause you to feel the pain of loss twice: first, you lock in your losses; then you risk missing out on the market's eventual recovery. This can leave a hole in your savings that never really gets repaired—you'll always have less savings to build on than if you stayed the course. Instead of fighting an exhausting battle with your emotions, develop a diversified long-term strategy and stick to it. After all, your long-term goals don't change overnight—so why should your portfolio?

Warren Buffett says that you should be fearful when people are greedy and greedy when others are fearful. If more of us had followed that advice before the crash, we'd all be better off. Many people wouldn't have bought that sixth or seventh investment property that seemed like too good a deal to pass up. Instead, we would have waited until prices dropped and scooped up properties on sale. That's exactly what a group of investors from California did here in Bend. When the real estate bubble burst, they swooped in and grabbed developed lots that hadn't been built on, paying as little as $20,000 each.

Just a few years later, they're getting $70,000 for those same pieces of land, more than tripling their money. I call that a killer return on investment.

We have two options when financial challenge hits. We can let emotion get the best of us. Or we can see the gift in adversity and be ready to take advantage of those shifts and seize opportunities that come our way.

LIFE IS 10 PERCENT WHAT HAPPENS TO YOU AND 90 PERCENT HOW YOU REACT

I was brought up with the ideology that some people say they can and some people say they can't. They are both right! It is imperative to stay positive during difficult times. No one said it better than Charles R. Swindoll:

The longer I live, the more I realize the impact of attitude on life. Attitude, to me, is more important than facts. It is more important than the past, than education, than money, than circumstances, than failure, than successes, than what other people think or say or do. It is more important than appearance, giftedness or skill. It will make or break a company... a church... a home. The remarkable thing is we have a choice everyday regarding the attitude we will embrace for that day. We cannot change our past... we cannot change the fact that people will act in a certain way. We cannot change the inevitable. The only thing we can do is play on the one string we have, and that is our attitude. I am convinced that life is 10 percent what happens to me and 90 percent of how I react to it. And so it is with you... we are in charge of our Attitudes.

I used to have this quote printed in miniscule print on the back of my business card as a reminder each day. I am convinced that the failures we experience are dress rehearsals for success

I started this book with a story about Mt. Everest and how once we get to the top of the mountain we are only half way into our journey with the most risky part of the journey still ahead of us. So it is only appropriate to end with a story about this legendary mountain.

George Mallory, a famous English mountaineer who took part in the first three British expeditions to Mt. Everest in the early 1920s, was once asked what the use of climbing Mt. Everest was. I find his response to be fitting today as we emerge from the Great Recession and reevaluate our core values and goals:

> *It is no use. There is not the slightest prospect of any gain whatsoever. We shall not bring back a single bit of gold or silver, not a gem, nor any coal or iron. We shall not find a single foot of earth that can be planted with crops to raise food. It's no use. So, if you cannot understand that there is something in man which responds to the challenge of this mountain and goes out to meet it, that the struggle is the struggle of life itself upward and forever upward, then you won't see why we go. What we get from this adventure is just sheer joy. And joy is, after all, the end of life. We do not live to eat and make money. We eat and make money to be able to enjoy life. That is what life means and what life is for.*

Unfortunately, on the third expedition, in June 1924, Mallory and his climbing partner Andrew Irvine both disappeared somewhere high on the Northeast Ridge.

Yes, there are risks to just about anything we do in life, but sometimes you just have to go for it. Only then can you truly be open to the opportunities in front of you. Only then can you tap into—and take advantage of—serendipity. Only then can you really live your life the way you want and deserve to.

So if you're ready to go for it, just do it! Along the way, don't forget to reach out for help when you need it. Together we can get you up and back down this financial mountain safely. Because as you climb toward retirement or enjoy those years you've worked so hard for, failure is simply not an option.

In Memory of
Ryan Robert Carlisle
May 10, 1976 - December 6, 2012

In memory of Ryan,

my incredible friend and business partner.

May endless sandy beaches always be yours, my friend.

Until we meet again.

ABOUT DAVID

My family and me, 2013.

D avid's inspiration and zest for life have been shaped by a lifetime of international travel and adventure.

With a current tally of more than 65 countries on four different continents, his quest for extreme travel has included hitchhiking through the Mekong Delta to Hanoi long before President Clinton's trade agreement helped to open the doors of Vietnam.

He spent three weeks climbing the infamous peaks of the Nepalese Himalayas, has lived tall amongst the pigmies of Uganda, and was one of the privileged to partake in tearing down the Berlin Wall.

As a recipient of a Retirement Distribution Certificate from the University of Pennsylvania's Wharton School of Business, David excels at turning his clients' IRAs and 401ks into *pay*checks and *play*checks. He has been featured in two of the financial industry's leading publications, *Financial Advisor* and *Financial Planning* magazine as well as on CNN Money, NPR and US News & World Report.

His company, Rosell Wealth Management, was a select finalist in 2008 for the management of the $500,000,000 Oregon 529 College Fund.

An accomplished speaker, David has addressed international audiences numbering in the thousands, including the Million Dollar Round Table®.

He's the past chairman of the Bend, Oregon, Chamber of Commerce and the City Club of Central Oregon. His life in Bend is closely documented by noted photographer Jill Rosell, his well-travelled wife from New Zealand, and constantly inspired by their two children Sophie and Jack.

The chief cause of failure and unhappiness is trading what you want most for what you want now.

—Zig Ziglar

For more information about personal finance —including videos, articles and other resources—go to www.RosellWealthManagement.com